The Cure

A Visual Documentary

by Dave Thompson & Jo-Ann Greene

Omnibus Press
London/Sydney/New York/Cologne

© Copyright 1988 Omnibus Press
(A Division of Book Sales Limited)
Edited by *Chris Charlesworth*
Art Direction by *Mike Bell*
Book Designed by *Peter Hodkinson*
Artwork by *Conway & Edginton*
Picture Research by *Mary McCartney*
Manuscript and project co-ordination by *Caroline Watson*

ISBN 0.7119.1387.0
Order No. OP44536

All rights reserved. No part of this book may be reproduced in any form or by any electronic or mechanical means, including information storage or retrieval systems, without permission in writing from the publisher, except by a reviewer who may quote brief passages.

Exclusive distributors:

Book Sales Limited
8/9 Frith Street,
London W1V 5TZ, UK.

Music Sales Corporation
225 Park Avenue South,
New York, NY 10003
USA.

Music Sales Pty. Limited
120 Rothschild Avenue,
Rosebery, NSW 2018,
Australia.

To the Music Trade only:
Music Sales Limited
8/9 Frith Street,
London W1V 5TZ, UK.

Picture credits:

All Action: 90.
Adrian Boot: 62.
Finn Costello: 38t, 40tl, 45b & 64b.
DiD Circle: 61.
London Features International: 2&3, 13, 22, 33, 37, 38b, 40bl, 41t, 43, 44, 45t, 48, 51, 52, 53, 56b, 57, 59, 60t, 63, 64tl, 69, 70, 71, 72, 73, 74, 75, 76, 77, 79, 80, 81, 84, 86, 87, 91 & 93.
Pictorial Press: 4, 52 (inset), 56t, 60bl & centre & br, 65, 68, 78, 88, 89, 92 & 94.
Andy Phillips: 32, 34 & 35.
Barry Plummer: 55 & 82.
Steve Rapport: 40tr & br & bc, 41b, 47, 49, 66 & 67.
Rex Features: Back cover, 57 (inset), 64tr, 83 & 85.
Relay Photos: 30.
Gabor Scott: 15, 17, 18, 19, 20, 24, 25, 36 & 39.
Ray Stevenson: 11, 23, 26 & 28.
Stills: Front cover.

Every effort has been made to trace the copyright holders of the photographs in this book but some were unreachable. We would be grateful if the photographers concerned would contact us.

Omnibus Press is grateful to the following for the loan of Cure memorabilia photographed for this book: Andrew Drage, Peter Horsted & Billy Wilson.

Typeset by Capital Setters, London.

Printed by Ebenezer Baylis & Son Limited, Worcester.

A catalogue record for this book is available from the British Library.

Introduction

The rise and rise of The Cure from unabashed cultdom to pop superstardom is one of modern rock's most welcome surprises. They were always guaranteed some attention, of course, whether struggling to shrug off the 'Southern Buzzcocks' tag which dogged them in their early days, or touring tirelessly behind an album that sounded like it was made in a church, but not until they had reached rock bottom, the end of the line, did things change.

A clutch of singles breached the Top 40, the Top 20, the Top 10. Suddenly The Cure were back in business, reports that they had split were hastily dismissed, complaints they had sold out were swiftly brushed aside. Without once losing touch with everything they were best at, The Cure suddenly erupted into pop culture consciousness; no longer a shadowy shape standing in the shadow of Top Of The Pops, suddenly they were out in the open, dancing, singing, smiling . . . all the things they once did in private were now dragged on to the world stage.

Yet through it all they retained all that was magic in the past; 'The Top' followed 'Pornography' as naturally as 'Love Cats' followed 'The Walk', outsiders might have placed new tags on The Cure, calling them enlightened, enlivened, but in their hypnotic basements of sound, the only thing that really changed was people's perception of what they were hearing.

And what are they hearing? Oh, nothing too special – only the sound of a band who come up fighting every time, who will never rest on their laurels simply because they never need to rest. Even at the end of another three month tour, tired and jaded though they must be feeling, there is a biting urgency about The Cure, a snarling impatience and a refusal to stand still. Every new record introduces another new facet; more than any other band around. The Cure are erecting new frontiers, constantly striving, constantly thriving.

Essentially The Cure's story is Robert Smith's story. He formed the band, he has led them through their many permutations. Until recently he wrote every song they recorded, and their genius is his genius. But at the same time it is only half the story. He has been weaving his spells for little more than a decade now. On the present evidence, his best work is still to come.

ROBERT JAMES SMITH was born in Blackpool on 21 April, 1959. "I remember bits of Blackpool . . . I'm sure that spending the first five years of your life by the sea means that you harbour a great love for the sea, because every time I have a holiday I always go to the sea. It's like it's calling me. I think I'd like to go and live by the sea.

"I grew up in the south rather than the north. I used to have a northern accent because my mum and dad used to talk like that at home. It always stuck out at school, which I never realised at the time. I thought everyone was saying 'grass' incorrectly. But I toned it down on purpose when I got into my teens. By then I think it might have been a bit pretentious to have affected a northern accent.

"My first really clear memory is arriving at Victoria Station in London on a steam train." Robert grew up in Crawley. "I still try to get back when I can – I've got my own room and bed and toothbrush there. It's really somewhere to escape to – it's impossible for people to get hold of me there if I don't answer the phone because they're not going to travel 35 miles, are they?"

He started school at St. Francis' primary, and it was there that he first met Lol Tolhurst. "He lived in the next street and we went to school on the same coach, but he made no impression on me whatsoever. He remembers me, though not very favourably." For the most part, his school reports said . . . "Something in the order of, I was doing less than I could. That was pretty accurate because at that time I was consciously trying to do as little as possible." His childhood ambition was to be the last human being in the world, which probably sums up how he felt getting up at 5.30 in the morning for his first job, sorting mail at the Post Office one Christmas while he was still at school.

"When I was 11 my school became the guinea pig for a project. It was called Notre Dame Middle School, a very free thinking experiment with open plan classrooms and stuff. It was hilarious, we really abused it. One day I wore a black velvet dress to school for a dare. It was the first time I got beaten up – by four kids on the way home. I'd worn it all day because the teachers just thought 'Oh it's a phase he's going through, he's got some kind of personality crisis, let's help him through it'."

At 14, Robert later said, his ambition was "to sit on top of a mountain and just die." Instead of that, he, his brother Richard, sister Janet, and some friends formed their first group, The Crawley Goat Band. "Then I had a group called The Group, because it was the only one at school so we didn't need a name. I never feel patronising towards anyone of 15, I remember still how I experienced things then. I could never write them down as well as I could at 25 . . . but I felt the same emotions, just as strong, in a much rougher form. Between 15 and 18 is when you develop your personality."

His early idols were disparate. Tommy Cooper, Spike Milligan, footballer Rodney Marsh and Alex Harvey. "Mary (Robert's girlfriend since they met in drama class, aged 14) and me used to follow him around the country. And he did nothing. I mean, everything was make believe, but he inspired two years of my life. Without him I'd have been into Supertramp, those sort of horrible groups. If I thought we had the same impact on people as The Sensational Alex Harvey Band had on me, I'd be . . . He was the only person that made me think, it must be fucking brilliant to be Alex Harvey. It was just like believing in a creature, a myth that was presented to you onstage."

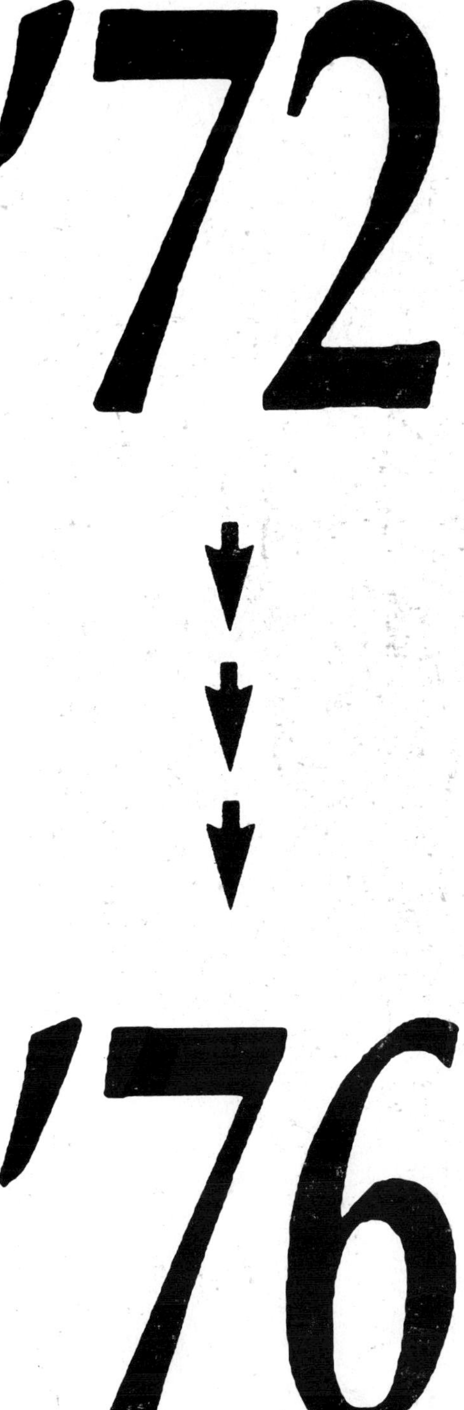

DECEMBER 1972

Robert receives his first electric guitar as a Christmas present, although he first began playing guitar "When I was six or seven. I was never very good." His teacher, Robert says, "was the gayest bloke I ever met [but] he never made a pass at me. He was so horrified by my playing, I think, that he couldn't bring himself to make a pass at me. He thought I had enough problems." From here on, Robert delights in skipping lessons to rehearse "weird versions" of current hits with a handful of like-minded friends – Lawrence 'Lol' Tolhurst, Michael Dempsey amongst them. The musical line-up was bizarre to say the least; instruments at the group's disposal included Spanish guitars, kettle drums and the school piano.

Towards the end of the next school year, the trio play their first gig, to their classmates, under the name of The Obelisks. Robert plays piano, Lol drums, Alan Hill bass, Michael and Marc Ceccagno guitars. It was, Robert later admits, "horrible".

"I lost my virginity when I was 15. I lost it with Mary. She was the nicest girl in the school. I went out with her because everyone else wanted to. We were at someone's party, a fancy dress party. I went as a surgeon. I remember because I poured all this tomato ketchup down me. At the time I thought it was a really good idea, but after an hour it really began to stink. Every time I moved I was completely overpowered by the sweet sickly smell of tomato ketchup . . . "

23 JANUARY 1976

Taking over the hall of St. Edwards Church in Crawley, Robert leads the band through their first proper rehearsal. He plays guitar, Michael Dempsey moves to bass, two long forgotten brothers handle drums and vocals. In the meantime, Lol is plucking up courage to take over the drum stool, and in April, replaces Graham, the original drummer.

Robert later reveals, "I've never told you about Lol have I? I've never told you the story of how we found him? Simon (Gallup) and I went on one of these school trips, y'know, educational holidays, to Africa and one day we discovered Lol in the bush. He'd been brought up by ant-eaters and half his face had been eaten off by ants. Well Simon and I, we felt sorry for him so we brought him back with us and paid for plastic surgery, fed him soup under piles of earth and all that, and how does he repay us? He sneaked ferrets under his skin, that's what he did, sneaked ferrets under the plastic surgery."

In October, with Marc Ceccagno having been replaced by Porl Thompson, Malice begin rehearsing their peculiar hybrids of old Bowie, Hendrix and Alex Harvey songs.

"When it first started I didn't have any objectives or ulterior motives other than not to have to work."

18 DECEMBER 1976

In the guise of a folk band, Malice play their first ever gig at Worth Abbey. They develop a purely acoustic set for the occasion.

20 DECEMBER 1976

Malice support Marc Ceccagno's new band, Amulet, at St. Wilfred's Comprehensive School in Crawley. Vocals were handled by a local journalist named Martin, and the set included 'Wild Thing' (sung by Lol), 'Suffragette City', 'Foxy Lady' and Thin Lizzy's 'Jailbreak'. Another song from this period, 'A Night Like This', is later revived by Robert for the 'Head In The Door' album.

"We pretended there was this jazz group and a choral quintet and sold about 150 tickets at 25p each. It turned into a riot."

JANUARY 1977

The year begins with Robert being expelled from school for being "an undesirable influence."

"I got reinstated, though – I got taken back but they never acknowledged I was there. It was hilarious. I did three A-Levels – failed Biology miserably, scraped through French and got a B in English. Then I spent eight or nine months on Social Security until they stopped my money.

"It came to the point where I'd rather have killed myself than get a job. I told Social Security to give the jobs to those who want them, I'd rather stay at home listening to music but they'd tell me I had to work and I'd just ask 'Why?'

"I brewed home-made lager so I shouldn't have to spend a lot of money drinking, which is a good hint for all you out-of-work people."

Also in January, the band rename themselves Easy Cure, after one of Lol's songs. Several vocalists file through the band's ranks, Martin having quit following the St. Wilfred's show.

APRIL 1977

The band spot an advert in one of the music papers, placed by Ariola-Hansa. It announces a talent contest, and Easy Cure – with Peter O'Toole (no relation!) now on vocals – record their entry on a tape recorder in Robert's front room. A few days later they receive a telegram, asking them to London for an audition.

6 MAY 1977

Easy Cure stand in for Amulet at The Rocket, a pub in Crawley. This eventually becomes the band's most regular haunt.

13 MAY 1977

Easy Cure arrive at Morgan Studios for their audition. They perform two of their own songs for the benefit of Hansa's video camera, and are offered a contract on the spot.

18 MAY 1977

The band sign for Hansa, despite suspicions that it was the band's image and looks which swayed the label's judgement, as opposed to their music. The previous year Hansa had thrown their all in with Child, a very suspect-looking brand of teenymeat whose every attempt to out-Roll the Rollers had come to grief. Easy Cure might not have been quite so good looking, but they were considerably more talented.

3 JUNE 1977

In the Queen's Jubilee Week, Easy Cure play a free Peace Concert in Queens Square, Crawley, and five days later receive their first ever press review, in the *Crawley Advertiser*. Over the next three months the band continue to play regularly, building up an enormous local following, but in September Peter O'Toole quits. Robert takes over from him as the band's singer.

"I've never really seen myself as a singer. In the

'ROCKING' TO THE TOP

A YOUNG Crawley based rock band, 'Easy Cure,' celebrated in Queens Square on Sunday, after signing a £1,000 contract the previous day.

The band, all aged between 18-19, was one of 1,400 bands to answer an advertisement in The Melody Maker music paper.

Only 60 bands were selected for an audition in London from which eight groups were offered a contract by Hansa, a leading German recording firm.

The group's first single will come out on the Antlantic record label.

"There were so many other bands that we didn't pin all our hopes on it," they said.

The group has only been together for eight months, and they have now signed a five-year contract, renewable every year.

One member, Robert Smith, said: "It all happened so fast, but now we are really looking forward to making our first record."

The group consists of Laurence Tolhurst, Mick Dempsey, Paul Thompson, Peter O'Toole and Robert Smith.

early days I never cared about giving a performance. I'd just work myself up into the state of mind needed for the song and that'd be it. Some of the things I sang were pretty good, but a lot of it was out of tune."

It is the summer of punk – The Adverts are looking through Gary Gilmore's eyes, The Jam are in the city, and the *NME*'s Ray Lowry sums up the pretenders to The Sex Pistols' throne with a cartoon which answers The Clash's demand for a White Riot with a daddy who responds, "Darling, I'll buy you one!" Says Robert, "We never felt part of that London orthodoxy. It was only really The Vibrators who speeded things up, particularly in contrast with the bands who were popular before, like The Dead. If you listen to a Sex Pistols record now, it's not that fast. We didn't throw away our old records because of punk."

Talking in 1981, Robert says, "The liberation of punk for us was the sense that you didn't have to be orthodox. It all began with a sense of total release, but you can't maintain that. There are still people playing that original punk style, people who've been left over in a time scale that stops there."

OCTOBER 1977
Using equipment purchased with the Hansa advance, the band record their first serious demo tape, comprising five songs: 'Meathook', 'See The Children', 'Pillbox Tales', 'I Want To Be Old' and 'I Just Need Myself'. A second tape, around a month later, includes 'Killing An Arab', 'I'm Cold', and three cover versions: 'I Saw Her Standing There', 'Rebel Rebel' and 'Little Girl'. However, Hansa reject all 10 and suggest the band try their hand at a few rock'n'roll numbers instead. The band ignore this advice, and in the early new year another session sees them produce versions of 'Rebel Rebel', 'Smashed Up', 'Plastic Passion' and 'I Just Need Myself'.

16 OCTOBER 1977
Felbridge Village Hall.

4 DECEMBER 1977
The Rocket, Crawley. One number from the band's set, 'Heroin Face', later turns up on the 'Curiosity' side of the 1984 live album, 'Concert'.

31 DECEMBER 1977
Orpington General Hospital.

19 FEBRUARY 1978
The band meet Simon Gallup at The Rocket, where he is playing bass with the evening's support band, Lockjaw.

MARCH 1978
The dispute with Hansa regarding Easy Cure's choice of material comes to a head when the band suggest 'Killing An Arab' is released as their first single. Hansa refuse, and by the end of the month, the contract has been dissolved.

"They just wanted us for what we looked like, not for our music, they didn't even listen to the demo tape we gave them. They just liked the photograph of ourselves we sent with it. They said even if 'Arab' was a good song they couldn't put it out because we had to keep in with the Arabs. It was so ridiculous."

It later turns out that Hansa's latest talent contest has turned up another bunch of pretty faces, Japan.

Below: On stage at Islington's Hope & Anchor in 1978. And if The Cure look cramped, imagine how Madness used to feel . . . Left to right: Robert, Lol and Michael.

The Cure

APRIL 1978
The band's sound begins to contract, courtesy of the Bon Tempi organ and Top 20 guitar (purchased from Woolworths for £20) which Robert has recently invested in. He claims the Top 20 is the best guitar he's ever had, and as proof reveals that he keeps a Fender Stratocaster in reserve. Meanwhile, however, Porl Thompson is feeling more and more ill at ease. His guitar sound clearly doesn't fit in with the rest of the group, and in early May he quit.

Around the same time, the remainder of the group decided to shorten their name – to The Cure.

27 MAY 1978
The group record four songs – 'Boys Don't Cry', '10.15 Saturday Night', 'Fire In Cairo' and 'It's Not You' – at a small local studio, and begin bombarding the major record companies with the resulting tape. Of these, the first named later appears on 'Curiosity'.

9 JULY 1978
The Cure put on a show at The Rocket, 'Mourning The Departed', designed as a memorial to Porl. Using a backing tape Robert recorded with an organ and an album of Church music, they held a seance on stage and Robert played the entire evening with a piece of wood nailed across his guitar so that it looked like a crucifix. At the end of the evening, Porl Thompson got up on stage and poured a pint of beer over Lol's head.

JULY 1978
Chris Parry, A&R man at Polydor, hears The Cure's tape and writes, asking to meet them.

14 JULY 1978
Brighton.

15 JULY 1978
Lakers Hotel, Redhill.

27 AUGUST 1978
Having met the band at the Polydor offices a fortnight earlier, Parry travels down to Redhill to see the band live at Lakers Hotel. After the show the party heads down to a nearby pub where Parry tells the group he is thinking of forming a record company of his own, which Polydor would distribute. He asks if they would be interested in becoming his first signing; they agree.

13 SEPTEMBER 1978
The Cure sign an initial six month deal with Fiction Records.

17 SEPTEMBER 1978
Lakers Hotel, Redhill.

20 SEPTEMBER 1978
The Cure return to Morgan Studios, this time with Parry in charge, to record five songs for their first album: 'Three Imaginary Boys', '10.15 Saturday Night', 'Fire In Cairo', 'Plastic Passion' and 'Killing An Arab'.

5 OCTOBER 1978
Support Wire at the Kent University, Canterbury. On the way home they crash the van into a wall.

6 OCTOBER 1978
A second show with Wire, at the London Polytechnic, is blown out after the band arrive too late to go on stage.

12 OCTOBER 1978
The Cure return to Morgan Studios, ensconcing themselves within for two days while they complete their album.

21 OCTOBER 1978
Lakers Hotel, Redhill.

25 OCTOBER 1978
Support The Young Bucks at The Windsor Castle.

28 OCTOBER 1978
Lakers Hotel, Redhill.

20 NOVEMBER 1978
Support the UK Subs at the Moonlight Club, West Hampstead.

24 NOVEMBER 1978
Town Hall, High Wycombe. The first night of the band's stint supporting Generation X, the group formed by Billy Idol and Tony James. Unable to pay for lighting or the PA, The Cure play with two standard lights on either side of them, and dig out their customary pub PA – two Yamaha A40 bins.

25 NOVEMBER 1978
Northampton Cricket Club with Generation X.

26 NOVEMBER 1978
Greyhound, Croydon.

28 NOVEMBER 1978
Top Rank, Cardiff.

30 NOVEMBER 1978
Halesowen Tiffanys.

1 DECEMBER 1978
Aston University, Birmingham.

2 DECEMBER 1978
West Runton Pavilion, Cromer.

3 DECEMBER 1978
Bristol Locarno.

4 DECEMBER 1978
The Cure make their début on the John Peel Show, performing 'Killing An Arab'.

5 DECEMBER 1978
California Ballroom, Dunstable. The last night of the tour. Although Generation X continue gigging until the end of the month, they do so without The Cure. Rumours fly concerning the split; one claims the headliners were jealous of the way The Cure went down every night, the other accuses Lol of urinating down Billy Idol's leg.

8 DECEMBER 1978
The Corn Dolly, Oxford. According to legend, the only song the audience want to hear is '10.15 Saturday Night', and The Cure end up playing nothing else.

11 DECEMBER 1978
Fan Club, Leeds.

12 DECEMBER 1978
Grey Hall, York.

13 DECEMBER 1978
Woods Leisure Centre, Colchester.

16 DECEMBER 1978
The Cure's first interview, with Adrian Thrills of the *New Musical Express*, is published under the title 'Ain't No Blues For The Summertime Cure'.

"Hands up those of you who still reckon you need expensive instruments to play rock'n'roll? I suggest you catch The Cure immediately." Robert tells him, "We see so many of the people we went to school with doing absolutely nothing. A lot of them are talented enough, but they just don't bother themselves. There are so many people playing music that is absolute rubbish and getting somewhere doing it. You just think 'if they're doing it, why don't you when you know you're so much better'."

19 DECEMBER 1978
The Hope And Anchor, Islington.

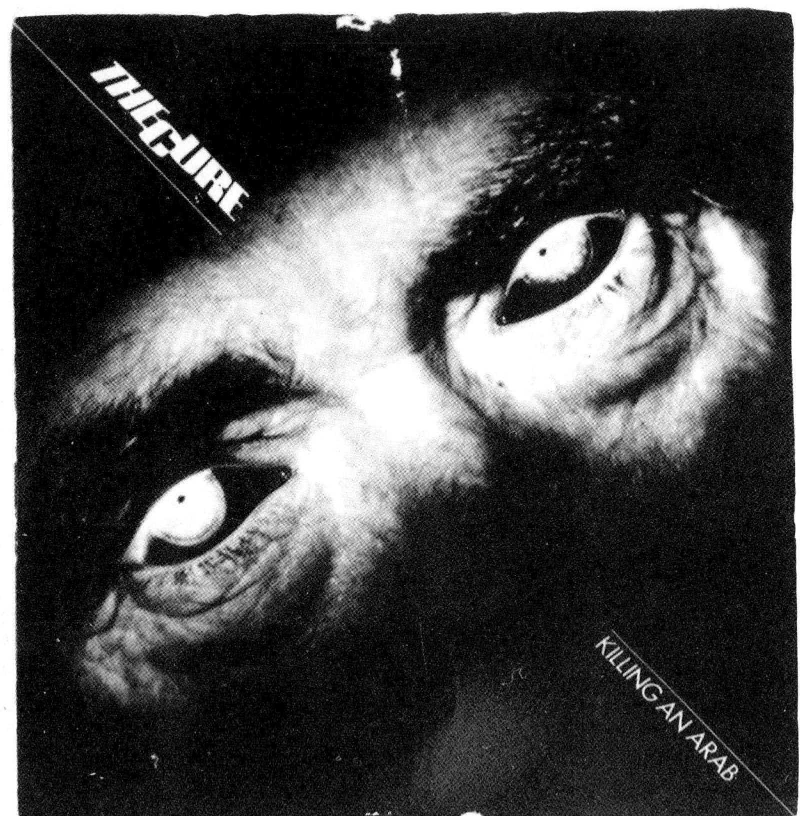

'79

22 DECEMBER 1978

The Cure celebrate the release of their first single, 'Killing An Arab'/'10.15 Saturday Night' with two gigs in one day. During the afternoon they play the Christmas party at Robert's dad's company, in the evening they support The Pirates at the Music Machine.

Although Fiction was all ready to go, the single was released on the independent Small Wonder label, primarily because Polydor were unwilling to release a record so close to Christmas. The deal was that Small Wonder, a tiny concern operating out of a record shop in Walthamstow, but nevertheless responsible for launching several bands on their way to later cult stardom, could press up to 15,000 copies of the single, after which Fiction would take over. Says Robert, "The single's a taster of what's to come. Small Wonder had initial orders of 2,000 so there was a lot of interest, people phoning up and things."

"Already an established live favourite, the release did much to pacify the cravings of the band's growing following, as well as fuelling the 'Southern Buzzcocks' tag which the Cure were rapidly acquiring in the eyes of the music press." (*Record Collector*).

"The thing about 'Killing An Arab' is that it is only a reference point in [our career], but it could have been a millstone. I can't understand it, but when people have an idea of the typical Cure sound, that's it. But that's just from that era. It's good that we got away from that sound because it could have killed us."

8 JANUARY 1979

The band return to Morgan Studios to continue work on the album, remaining there for the next month, but emerging occasionally to play shows. One, at the Moonlight Club in West Hampstead, earns the band even more accolades from the press.

"They kick into 'It's Not You' and I'm surprised. The sound is not at all the new-musical squeal that maybe I'd subconsciously expected. Very poppy, but still kept low-key and clipped to the bare essentials. They follow with 'Boys Don't Cry' and again your attention is held tight to what's going on . . . Like the early and late lamented Buzzcocks, nothing is spared, the whole set is minimal glory . . . Robert's lead is killing but it's that bass sound that steals the evening's honours, Mick using it like a lead instrument and pushing the whole sound along quite nicely." (*Sounds*).

"The songs mesh a stylishly understated plundering of classic sixties pop rock with post-punk economy and drive. The effect is tight and open-ended, considered but on the right side of rough." (*Melody Maker*).

13 JANUARY 1979

Sounds becomes the first British music paper to review 'Killing An Arab'. "'Killing An Arab' is unfair in a way as a record. OK. The, ah, A-side (well, the side that gives you the impression of being the A-side) is nice and fresh and crisp and funny. Quaint. You immediately love it." Of the B-side, Dave McCullouch continues, "It hits upon the value of sparseness in rock'n'roll like no other record has in oh, as far back as I can think. There's scarcely any playing in the song at all. Everything is left to your imagination."

20 JANUARY 1979
Melody Maker add their voice to the growing acclaim for 'Killing An Arab'. "As 'Hong Kong Garden' used a simple oriental-styled riff to striking effect, so 'Arab' conjures up edginess through a Moorish-flavoured guitar pattern."

27 JANUARY 1979
Sounds publish Dave McCullouch's interview with the band, titled 'Kill Or Cure'. The band also appear on the magazine's cover.

"Who are they, what are they, what do they look like, am I going to be disappointed?"

The interview took place in the Natural History Museum, at the band's insistence.

"They look so young it's not true. Robert resplendent in baggy, singularly silly and unhip pants. He's skinny and alarmingly handsome. They look younger in the way that most grammar school kids from fairly safe family backgrounds look younger. Unexposed and clean." The band themselves, McCullouch writes, are "Very musical. Almost rootless. The Cure brought back the spark of rock'n'roll to me. Youth. Energy. Endless potential and hope."

3 FEBRUARY 1979
Sounds claim the band were gobbed on by Skinheads because of their "blow-waves and baggies."

9 FEBRUARY 1979
The Nashville, West Kensington. The band's performance is marred by the attention of the National Front, who have perceived 'Killing An Arab' (reissued today on Friction) to be about just that, and who are distributing leaflets to that effect. In reality, it was based on a short novel by the French writer, Albert Camus, although the NF's confusion was easy to understand. Lol himself later revealed that, opening the curtains of his hotel room one morning he saw an Arab standing in the car park four floors below, staring up at him. "I thought he was going to pull out a shotgun."

23 FEBRUARY 1979
The Village, Newport.

27 FEBRUARY 1979
Metro, Plymouth.

28 FEBRUARY 1979
Town Hall, Bournemouth. The following morning the local paper features the headline 'MAN LOSES EAR AT POP CONCERT' after a girl pulled her boyfriend's ear off during The Cure's set.

MARCH 1979
Polydor release the '20 Of A Different Kind' compilation album, which features 'Killing An Arab' alongside contributions from The Adverts, Otway-Barrett, Sham 69 and a host of lesser lights.

1 MARCH 1979
Boogie House, Norwich.

2 MARCH 1979
Isleworth Poly, Hounslow.

3 MARCH 1979
Plough Inn, Cheltenham.

4 MARCH 1979
The Marquee, London. The first of a four week, Sunday night, residency. The Scars, Local Operator, Fashion and Joy Division comprise the support bands, and admission is £1 a night.

8 MARCH 1979
Hounslow Borough College.

11 MARCH 1979
The Marquee, London.

13 MARCH 1979
Oxford Poly.

14 MARCH 1979
Pop Club, York.

15 MARCH 1979
Fan Club, Leeds.

16 MARCH 1979
Sandpiper, Nottingham.

17 MARCH 1979
University Of Kent, Canterbury.

18 MARCH 1979
The Marquee, London.

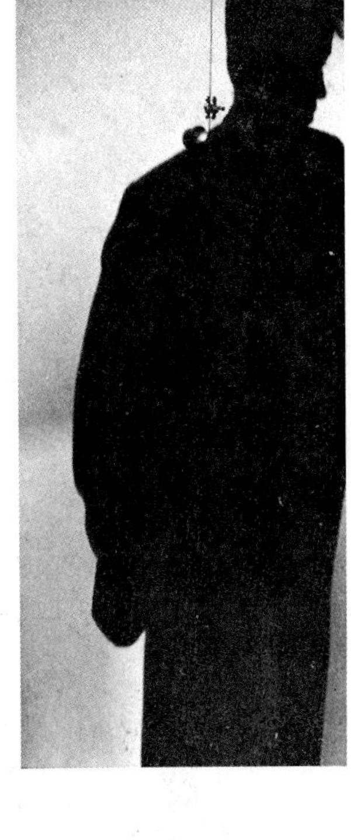

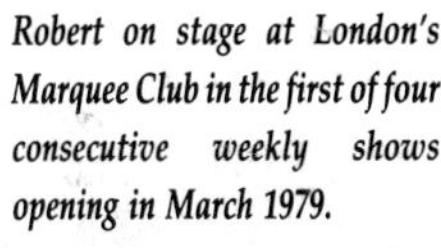

Robert on stage at London's Marquee Club in the first of four consecutive weekly shows opening in March 1979.

The Cure

20 MARCH 1979
Huddersfield Poly.

22 MARCH 1979
Conway Hall, London.

23 MARCH 1979
West Runton Pavilion, Cromer.

24 MARCH 1979
Eric's, Liverpool. *Melody Maker* run Ian Birch's interview with the band. Robert tells writer Ian Birch, "You can do much more with less instruments. That's why the single sounds different. If someone else had done it, they would probably have thought it needed a keyboard or a rhythm guitar playing along with the bass. Because it hasn't got that, people think 'Ah, there's something wrong because it sounds slightly unbalanced'."

Michael Dempsey says, "Pretence is presenting yourself in a way that you don't like, or that you find over the top. Presentation, on the other hand, is just the way you are. I'd like to think that we have a little more integrity, a little more honesty to present ourselves the way we are, rather than present an image. We're our only yardstick."

In a later interview, Robert explains, "The reason for the non-image was that, as a group, we weren't particularly affiliated with anything. There was no left wing, no right wing, no nothing. People think that if you're in a group and you enjoy playing the same sort of music, you have to have the same beliefs or like the same things or stand for the same things. I don't think it really follows. If it was a co-operative like The Mekons, I could understand it, but with us it's just a musical thing. I don't really socialise with Mick or Lol. I never socialise with anyone really."

In another interview he complained, "We had to get away from that anti-image thing, which we didn't even create in the first place. And it seemed like we were trying to be even more obscure. We just didn't like that standard rock thing. The whole thing got really out of hand. I hated that time around then. I was trying really hard to be normal, at home I was being all nice and my mum kept saying to me, 'What's an anti-image?'"

The accompanying photographs are taken on Clapham Common, outside UK Sub Charlie Harper's house. "But they made us look like a bunch of tramps so Bill (Chris Parry) decided we needed to look a bit more 'up market'. He gave us about £50 each to go out and buy 'some decent clothes'."

Their next session, with photographer Sheila Rock, has Robert and Lol kitted out in Miss Selfridge jackets.

25 MARCH 1979
The Marquee, London.

30 MARCH 1979
Pavilion, West Runton.

3 APRIL 1979
Technical College, Chippenham.

5 APRIL 1979
Chesterfield Fusion Hall, the first gig at that venue since the Pink Floyd in 1968. At the hotel after the show, a police raid leads to the arrest, on drug charges, of one of the band's road crew.

6 APRIL 1979
Watford College.

7 APRIL 1979
"The Cure may be a hype, but it may also be three young people geared in the same direction, creating not a new form or attitude for and towards rock and roll, but refocusing some of its more vital elements, forcing the observer to adjust his stance, to think and enjoy . . . The Cure are about precision, tempered and channelled energy, ideas and provocation of thoughts. They are not an essential life force. They are merely good." (*Record Mirror*).

29 APRIL 1979
Northgate Community Centre, Crawley, supported by Amulet. The show is a benefit for an old school-teacher friend of Robert and Lol's, whose homosexuality has lost him several teaching posts.

5 MAY 1979
The Cure's first album, '3 Imaginary Boys', is released by Fiction. As if to emphasise the band's total lack of image, the cover depicts nothing more than a lampstand, a fridge and a Hoover. Three imaginary household objects, whose appearance Michael later denigrates in an interview with *NME*. "It was someone else's idea and it proved only detrimental to us. We had kids coming up and asking us to explain our album and we couldn't. How do you explain someone else's artwork? It's impossible, and that's when our prefabricated image began to crumble."

The album goes on to spend three weeks in the chart, peaking at number 44. Reviews, for the most part, are complimentary, although Paul Morley in the *NME* is not impressed. Indeed, so vitriolic are his words that the band rewrite the lyrics of 'Grinding Halt' for him next time they appear on the John Peel show.

"Aah! More alert and anguished young men chalking up more sanctional and sanctimonious marks. Do not applaud them. [The album] contains 12 self-conscious variations upon a smoothly quirky theme . . . The Cure are trying to tell us something. They are trying to tell us they don't exist."

Neither are the band too happy with the album, particularly singling out the production, by Mike Hedges and Chris Parry. "If we'd produced it ourselves it would have sounded completely different. It would have been much softer and maybe it wouldn't have had as much impact. So it was good in a way that Chris did produce it, because it threw a perspective on the songs that we'd never seen before and so we could always see how we wanted to develop."

Six years later Robert says, "I hardly ever listen to any of our old stuff now. Once the songs have been recorded and put on vinyl they are someone else's entertainment, and not ours."

"The Cure is a three-piece with a minimalist approach that resembles both the early Talking Heads (when it, too, was a trio) and Wire. Like both those groups, The Cure concern themselves with creating sound paintings using the barest palette available - one guitar, bass, drums and voice - within the framework of the rock'n'roll band format. And like those bands they don't try to overpower where others might overdub, smother with power chords or merely turn up the volume. Instead they create a tension by the thinness, an hypnotic atmosphere which gives the music a trance-like power which seems to override just about everything else in importance. Listening to '3 Imaginary Boys', one can forget things like melodies and lyrics and just get caught up in the flow of the music." (*Trouser Press*).

The album preserves for posterity the bulk of The Cure's current live set, although the absence of 'Killing An Arab' does tend to detract from the overall strength of the set, at least as far as the window-shopper is concerned. In its stead, The Cure's bizarre interpretation of Jimi Hendrix's 'Foxy Lady' gives rise to some comment: "Imagine Hendrix without the guitar flash, phasing and stereo trickery and you're left with a sparse, twitching skeleton." (*Sound International*).

12 MAY 1979
All three leading music papers review the album. Shortly after, white labels of Lol's 'Grinding Halt' are pressed up as a possible second single, but apart from a review in the *New Musical Express*, response is poor and the idea is dropped. Wrote Ian Penman, "The Cure's particular hypothesis concerns a situation of non-forward moving national community activity. Got that? This is the sort of thing we in the Brill Building call a 'hype'."

17 MAY 1979
Memorial Hall, Northwich.

18 MAY 1979
Village, Newport.

19 MAY 1979
Good Mood Club, Halifax. In the *NME*, Nick Kent writes, "They are not rude or particularly cliquish, but the interviewer senses that the ongoing interview situation is not one that they feel particularly at home with, that they find the process bemusing, almost quaint in its ridiculousness. As personalities, drummer Tolhurst appears the most democratic and business-like, while guitarist Smith, definitely older than his age, is the creative shoulder-shrugging one. Between this pair, bassist Dempsey blends in without adding any particular dimension . . . [However] what will follow may well be some of the finest pop of the eighties."

In answer to the first of these accusations, that The Cure do not like interviews, Robert later says, "You put out an album that's greeted with some measure of critical acclaim and you're immediately in a position where people should listen to you. It might be flattering to know that people want to know what you think, but I don't really see myself as one of the top three original thinkers in the world today, so I'm not in any position to expound my philosophy of life."

21 MAY 1979
Top Of The World, Stafford.

22 MAY 1979
Barbarellas, Birmingham.

23 MAY 1979
Stowaway, Newport.

24 MAY 1979
Routes, Exeter.

25 MAY 1979
Portsmouth Poly.

26 MAY 1979
Civic Hall, Totnes.

28 MAY 1979
Camelot Suite, Yeovil.

29 MAY 1979
Limit Club, Sheffield. "Their biography puts their age at 20; they look younger and write songs which are presumably intended to imply they're older. Not their fault, I suppose. The end result, which is their fault, is that they fall slap bang into the third (predominant) category, that of being mutton dressed as lamb." (*New Musical Express*).

31 MAY 1979
Boogie House, Norwich

1 JUNE 1979
Carshalton Park. Misguided Mod revivalists The Merton Parkas and Secret Affair are also on the bill. Robert later reveals that it was the Mod revival, which was born out of nothing more than the release of The Who's *Quadrophenia* movie, and a few misguided remarks from Paul Weller, which inspired 'Jumping Someone Else's Train'.

2 JUNE 1979
Whitcombe Lodge, Cheltenham.

4 JUNE 1979
Tiffanys, Nottingham.

5 JUNE 1979
Huddersfield Poly.

7 JUNE 1979
Eric's, Liverpool.

8 JUNE 1979
Lafayette, Wolverhampton.

9 JUNE 1979
Manchester Poly.

11 JUNE 1979
Crawford Arms, Milton Keynes.

12 JUNE 1979
Circles, Swansea.

13 JUNE 1979
Crocs, Rayleigh.

14 JUNE 1979
Fusion, Chesterfield.

15 JUNE 1979
AJs, Lincoln.

16 JUNE 1979
University Of Kent, Canterbury.

17 JUNE 1979
Lyceum, London. "No Hoover, fridge or lamp shade on stage, just a nice fat ventilator to keep them cool and casual. And further fine hardware in the form of attractive lights beaming blue and yellow on the band and white on the audience. Did you know they were the Pink Floyd of the new wave? Halfway through 1979 and The Cure can consider themselves prime contenders for the Most Frustrating Band Of The Year award . . . " (*Record Mirror*).

26 JUNE 1979
'Boys Don't Cry'/'Plastic Passion' is released as The Cure's second single.

"Brings to mind the image of John Lennon at 12 or 13." (*Record Mirror*).

"In a perfect world, that'd have been number one," Robert later says, although he adds in another interview, that if it had been a hit he would have been forced to rewrite it again and again to try and maintain the success. He is glad, therefore, that it failed. Finally, he reveals, "Paul Young was going to do 'Boys Don't Cry' and they asked us for our blessing and we said no. I can't think of anything worse."

28 JUNE 1979
Troubadour, Port Talbot.

29 JUNE 1979
Lafayette, Wolverhampton.

30 JUNE 1979
Aylesbury Friars, supporting Wire.

JULY 1979
Robert 'discovers' The Obtainers, two pre-teenagers who played Tupperware boxes and pots and pans. Robert releases a single by them, 'Yeah Yeah Yeah', on his own Dance Fools Dance label, with a track by The Mag Spies, featuring Simon Gallup, on the flip.

"The first thing Simon bought me was 'I'm A Moody Guy' by Shane Fenton and the Fentones, because he thought I was a moody bastard. He posted it through my letterbox. In half. So I've never actually heard it, but it's my favourite record."

1 JULY 1979
The Cure headline the London Lyceum. The Ruts support.

5 JULY 1979
Barbarellas, Birmingham.

6 JULY 1979
The Factory, Manchester.

29 JULY 1979
The Cure play their first foreign date, an outdoor festival in Holland.

AUGUST 1979
"There's a new sort of sound evolving amongst some of the new English bands, characterised by steady drumbeats, well-defined loping bass lines and guitar used to punctuate or underline. The lyrics are about non-love, the absence of love and about quasi-military violence, i.e. various forms of alienation. The Mekons, their brother band The Gang Of Four and The Cure are the three foremost

Michael Dempsey on stage at London's Lyceum, July 1979. After this concert Robert criticised the choice of support act – The Ruts – by claiming the promoters cared nothing for compatibility.

proponents of the style, each in their own way . . ." (*Trouser Press*).

3 AUGUST 1979
At a Throbbing Gristle concert in London, Robert meets Steve Severin of fellow Polydor band, Siouxsie And The Banshees, who immediately invites The Cure to join the forthcoming Banshees' tour.

24 AUGUST 1979
The Cure play the first night of the annual Reading Festival. The Tourists, The Police and Motorhead (to whom Robert dedicates 'Boys Don't Cry') and Wilko Johnson are also on the bill.

"A music with all the substance of candy floss and none of the sweetness . . . Three infuriating berks." (*New Musical Express*).

29 AUGUST 1979
Stateside Theatre, Bournemouth. The opening night of a tour supporting Siouxsie And The Banshees.

30 AUGUST 1979
Aylesbury Friars. "It wasn't until the last number that I remembered what all the fuss was about earlier this year . . . It ('Killing An Arab') still sounds good but it stood out tonight as a fluke – a momentary flash of brilliance not repeated in anything else The Cure have done." (*New Musical Express*).

SEPTEMBER 1979
As Michael Dempsey grows more unhappy with the style of songs Robert is writing, The Cure go into the studio to record their third single, 'Jumping Someone Else's Train'/'I'm Cold'. Siouxsie, of the Banshees, helps out on backing vocals on the latter.

5 SEPTEMBER 1979
Ulster Hall, Belfast. At the show it turns out the band's equipment hasn't yet arrived and The Cure end up playing after the headliners, using borrowed equipment.

Robert: "Until the Banshees tour we'd never really been a support act, and on that one we were more like special guests. There were usually three bands on and we didn't wanna be, like, the Banshees' support group."

6 SEPTEMBER 1979
In Aberdeen, the Banshees are ripped apart when drummer Kenny Morris and guitarist John McKay quit with no warning, hours before the band are due to take the stage. The problem arose after the band trooped down to a local record store, where they were due to make an appearance, signing copies of their latest album, 'Join Hands'. Unfortunately Polydor, the band's record label, had seriously under-estimated the support the band could command in the area – the shop ordered 200 copies of the album, Polydor delivered just 50, all of which were sold within moments of the band walking into the shop. Fortunately the Banshees manager, Nils, had a pile of albums in the back of his car. He sold them to the shop owner, but Morris and McKay took it upon themselves to then start handing the albums out for free. When the shop owner remonstrated with them, the pair announced they wouldn't sign any more autographs. Siouxsie and Severin tried to restore order, but an argument developed and Morris and McKay stormed out. By the time the rest of the entourage returned to the hotel, the pair were already on a train back to London, their tour passes pinned to their pillows.

That night, The Cure's set is extended after the remaining Banshees, Siouxsie and Severin, have explained the situation to the crowd, and the show ended with the pair joining The Cure onstage for a version of the headliners' show-stopper, 'The Lord's Prayer'.

After the show, Robert offers to take over guitar duties in the Banshees, besides playing with The Cure, for the duration of the tour. In the meantime, shows at Glasgow Apollo (September 8), Dunfermline Kinnema (September 9), Bradford St.Georges Hall (September 12), Oxford New Theatre (September 14) are cancelled.

8 SEPTEMBER 1979
Sounds' David Hepworth complains, "Had there been a handy exit I'm sure I would have used it. Smith, who was inhabiting some lurid green suit that looked like a cross between a bull-fighter's costume and a Charlie Cairoli cast-off, floated across the bar like a man who is just too damned effete to live, offered a hand like a portion of under-cooked haddock, asked if there was anything non-alcoholic to drink, simpered that the rest of the band couldn't make it and then leaned wanly against the wall and made only token efforts to return my pathetic attempts at conversation."

10 SEPTEMBER 1979
The Cure headline the Rotterdam New Pop Festival in front of 10,000 people.

18 SEPTEMBER 1979
The Banshees tour resumes at the DeMontfort Hall, Leicester. After an appeal broadcast on the John Peel Show turns up hundreds of potential replacements for the errant pair, none of whom are actually any good, Robert is installed as guitarist, Budgie (from The Slits) as drummer. "Smith has a task which would have daunted lesser players; after first coming on with his own lot he's gotta abruptly change guitar and mood to play an unfamiliar act. But he handles this enforced schizophrenia with the minimum of fuss, and armed with new guitar and flanger (to get that swishing McKay tone) comes out on top, cautious but convincing." (*New Musical Express*).

The band are joined on tour by *NME* writer Deanne Pearson, who reveals that Lol also offered his services, as drummer, to the Banshees should the need arise. However, her biggest coup is in pointing out Michael Dempsey's growing unhappiness. "I don't want people to think of The Fatman (Lol) and I as the Bruce Foxton and the Rick Buckler of the band, the two jokers. We're not really silly all the time."

19 SEPTEMBER 1979
Odeon, Birmingham.

21 SEPTEMBER 1979
Apollo, Manchester.

22 SEPTEMBER 1979
Winter Gardens, Malvern.

23 SEPTEMBER 1979
Hippodrome, Bristol.

24 SEPTEMBER 1979
St. Georges Hall, Bradford.

25 SEPTEMBER 1979
Sophia Gardens, Cardiff.

26 SEPTEMBER 1979
New Theatre, Oxford.

27 SEPTEMBER 1979
Odeon, Taunton.

28 SEPTEMBER 1979
Gaumont, Southampton.

29 SEPTEMBER 1979
Pavilion, Hemel Hempstead.

30 SEPTEMBER 1979
Empire, Liverpool.

1 OCTOBER 1979
Nottingham University. A version of 'Subway Song', recorded at this show, later appears on 'Curiosity'.

3 OCTOBER 1979
City Hall, Newcastle.

4 OCTOBER 1979
Carlisle.

8 OCTOBER 1979
City Hall, Hull.

9 OCTOBER 1979
Gaumont, Ipswich.

10 OCTOBER 1979
Conference Centre, Brighton.

11 OCTOBER 1979
Odeon, Chelmsford.

13 OCTOBER 1979
Odeon, Lewisham.

15 OCTOBER 1979
Odeon, Hammersmith. Final night of the tour. "I think The Banshees and the roadies and everyone think we're rather silly and naïve at times because we all get so excited about things. Sometimes I smile, like when Budgie and I make mistakes we look at each other and grin. We can't help it, but that's not the Banshees' image is it? They're supposed to be all deep and dark and brooding."

NOVEMBER 1979
Following the completion of the Banshees' tour, Michael Dempsey quits The Cure, admitting later that he felt he was holding back The Cure's set. Robert is already writing material for the band's second album – he had, in fact, débuted some of it at the Aberdeen show in September – and Michael knows he has no place in a band which sounds like that! He is replaced in the line-up by Simon Gallup. Mag Spies keyboard player Matthieu Hartley joins at the same time.

The same month, Fiction release a single, 'I'm A Cult Hero'/'I Dig You', recorded by Robert and Simon, and released under the name The Cult Heroes. Lol, Porl Thompson, a postman named Frank (who sings on the track) and Robert's sister, Janet, join them on the tracks. The single eventually sold 35,000 copies in Canada, although it did nothing elsewhere.

2 NOVEMBER 1979
'Jumping Someone Else's Train'/'I'm Cold' released.

10 NOVEMBER 1979

Michael Dempsey tells the *NME*, "I suppose you could call it a clash of personalities, but I was definitely booted out and I'm looking for another gig." After rumours that he was to form a new band with Porl Thompson, Michael eventually joins The Associates, another band managed by Chris Parry. Robert later says, prior to Dempsey's departure, The Cure had been little more than "three people who just met once a week to play for enjoyment. It just became like a job. I'd known Lol since I was six, but not Michael. The differences were between him and me. The more it went on, the more unbearable it became. I found on The Banshees tour that I was enjoying playing with The Banshees more than I was with The Cure. That's what really made the decision. Lol felt the same way; Michael wasn't criticising or joining in on any level. We were getting really sort of banal. We were sticking to the same set night after night and the whole thing was getting like a joke. None of us were enjoying it, there wasn't much point in carrying on."

16 NOVEMBER 1979

The new look Cure début at Liverpool Eric's, the first night of the Future Pastimes Tour. The Associates and The Passions support. Of the new arrivals in the band's ranks Robert tells *Record Mirror*, "We were actually beginning to feel like a group. If you're in a band and you're playing together for a concentrated period of time you have to get on with each other – unless you're only in it for the money, which we're not. It's not so much the unity of thinking, because everybody thinks differently, but the unity of ideas. There's respect for everybody else's ideas. If someone thinks something they say it. And despite what the press think there's no hierarchy in The Cure. If there's one drink on the table we all fight for it."

Left to right – Robert, Lol, Simon, Matthieu.

On stage at The Music Machine, London, December 1979.

17 NOVEMBER 1979
London School Of Economics.

20 NOVEMBER 1979
Preston Polytechnic.

21 NOVEMBER 1979
Manchester University.

22 NOVEMBER 1979
Palm Cove, Bradford.

23 NOVEMBER 1979
The Village, Newport.

24 NOVEMBER 1979
Warwick University, Coventry.

27 NOVEMBER 1979
Sheffield University.

28 NOVEMBER 1979
Birmingham University.

29 NOVEMBER 1979
Portsmouth Polytechnic.

30 NOVEMBER 1979
University Of East Anglia, Norwich.

1 DECEMBER 1979
Durham University.

5 DECEMBER 1979
Wolverhampton Polytechnic.

6 DECEMBER 1979
Music Machine, London.

7 DECEMBER 1979
Crawley College, the last night of the tour. "It was good fun in the bus but it wasn't so much fun in the concerts. We gradually fell out and actually came to blows with The Passions. The Associates were always on our side. Apart from Clair (vocalist) The Passions were always very difficult – they had very peculiar ideologies."

Following the completion of the tour, The Cure head for the continent again for an 11-date tour, including three shows in Eindhoven, Amsterdam and Paris.

13 JANUARY 1980
Sessions for the band's second album commence at Morgan Studios. Robert chooses to produce, with Mike Hedges.

15 JANUARY 1980
The band take time off from the album sessions to fulfil a Dutch engagement. A version of 'In Your House', recorded here is later included on 'Curiosity'.

MARCH 1980
Somewhat belatedly, the American magazine *Trouser Press* reviews 'Jumping Someone Else's Train'. "Another outfit that just keeps getting better, and stays unpredictable to boot. On their third single they find a middle ground between the wall-eyed starkness of the first and the mellifluous melody of the second. Rapidly locomotivating bass and drums, and bile soaked vocals are offset by delicate, bittersweet guitar. 'Train' rides into the run off grooves over a jarring, percussive clattering."

Outside the BBC TV studios in Shepherds Bush, April 1980, waiting their turn to appear on Top Of The Pops immediately after Michael Dempsey quit. "We weren't compatible," said Robert. "And he didn't like the songs I was writing."

18 MARCH 1980
The Lakeside, Crawley. Porl Thompson joins the band onstage for an encore of 'I'm A Cult Hero'.

23 MARCH 1980
The Cult Heroes play their first, and only gig, supporting The Passions at the Marquee. Robert, Lol, Matthieu and Simon are joined by Porl, postman Frank and two schoolgirls. Apart from both sides of the single, the band's set comprises the complete Top 10 of five years previous: 'Do You Wanna Touch Me', 'Blockbuster', 'Whisky In The Jar', '20th Century Boy', 'Cindy Incidentally', 'Part Of The Union', 'Feel The Need In Me', 'Hello Hooray' . . .

APRIL 1980
Robert joins The Associates in the studio to perform backing vocals on several numbers from their forthcoming album. Later in the month, Matthieu Hartley tells *Record Mirror* readers where each member of the band would most like to live: "Mine would be a vegetable garden I could eat my way through forever. Simon's town would have everything made of leather, even the houses and inflatable wimps you could chain to your legs and kick as you went along. Tolhurstville was a long street with a sweet shop, then a pub, then a toilet, then the same again and again into infinity. Robert's place would be full of people in separate rooms sitting and staring at walls."

Meanwhile the Banshees are working on their latest album, with John McGeoch now installed as guitarist. At least one song on the set, 'Hybrid', was – says Siouxsie – formulated while Robert was a member of the band.

Robert, on stage with Siouxsie & The Banshees.

3 APRIL 1980
Robert guests onstage with The Stranglers at the Finsbury Park Rainbow, playing guitar in an all-star line-up protesting at the imprisonment of Strangler Hugh Cornwell on a drugs charge.

5 APRIL 1980
'A Forest'/'Another Journey By Train' released as a single. The A-side is taken from the forthcoming '17 Seconds' album, the B-side is an instrumental progression from 'Jumping Someone Else's Train', and the two numbers are often segued together in the band's live set. Julie Burchill, in the *NME*, reviews the single by accusing the band of "Trying to stretch a sketchy living out of moaning more meaningfully than any man has ever moaned before . . . without a tune, too."

10 APRIL 1980
The Cure arrive in the United States for their first tour. They play just three cities, opening at Emerald City, Cherry Hill, NJ.

"They took the stage more than a little jet-lagged, but seemingly quite sure of themselves, opening with two songs that no-one in the US has ever heard before, '17 Seconds' followed by 'Play For Today'. [They] then alternated between the older, poppier songs and the new material, which in the studio version sounds mechanised and heavy on the continental angst, but live packs a great droning wallop." (*Melody Maker*).

15-17 APRIL 1980
Hurrahs, New York. Robert later told *Record Mirror* that America was all about "people who all asked the same questions and all want to shake your hand. You just find yourself getting sucked into the whole rock'n'roll trip."

21 APRIL 1980
The Underground Club, Boston. It is Robert's 21st birthday, and to celebrate, the band come on stage almost an hour and a half late. Robert then breaks his thumb changing the wheel on the van on the way to the airport.

24 APRIL 1980
The Cure make their début on Top Of The Pops, performing 'A Forest', which entered the UK chart on 12 April. "I just couldn't believe how boring it was being on it," Robert admits. "You know the people who go 'whoop whoop', I really hate them. I have to be physically restrained sometimes." The single eventually peaks at number 31.

"The perfect pop song, the all-time classic." (*Sounds*).

25 APRIL 1980
Cromer, West Runton Pavilion, opening night of The Cure's latest British tour.

26 APRIL 1980
Osborne Club, Manchester. '17 Seconds' is reviewed in the British music press and generally decried for its coldness. Simon later tells *Sound International*, "Our aim on the album was to create a mood. Not a series of moods, but different aspects of one mood."

"I liked '17 Seconds'," says Robert. "I much preferred it to '3 Imaginary Boys'. There were only so many songs on the first album because they were drawn from two years before we recorded it. The songs we always preferred were '3 Imaginary Boys' itself, 'Accuracy' and '10.15 Saturday Night'. If they'd been expanded, any of those songs could have fit on '17 Seconds'. As it was, most of the songs were really embryonic, they were just put down. They were very naive. It worked in that way, but the whole thing was too much like a compilation album."

He tells *Record Mirror*, "I knew what I wanted it to sound like, the general mood. There's no point in trying to intellectualise about it because it's a genuine emotion that's on the LP. There was no policy, just that it turned out like that and I was aware beforehand that a lot of reviews would by-pass the emotion and just concentrate on the reasons for it turning out [like it did]. The whole point about the band is that we've been completely unpredictable so far, that we haven't been going in the same direction all along, that the next set of songs will probably turn out completely different. We happen to breed different styles, different phases. It takes some bands years to move through new musical corridors, but with us . . . "

"For anyone expecting '17 Seconds' to be a collection of great pop music, the joke is definitely

on them . . . Indeed, '17 Seconds' is far more oblique in its arrangement and construction than '3 Imaginary Boys' could ever have been. The sleeve is littered with blurred, out of focus shots, while the record itself makes no concessions to alerting the listener to The Cure's current pitch." (*NME*).

"Why don't The Cure come out of their shell? Why don't they come out to play? This is a reclusive, disturbed Cure, sitting in cold, dark empty rooms, watching clocks." (*Record Mirror*).

27 APRIL 1980
Locarno, Bristol.

28 APRIL 1980
Stateside Centre, Bournemouth.

29 APRIL 1980
Tiffanys, Coventry.

30 APRIL 1980
Top Rank, Brighton.

1 MAY 1980
Hull University.

2 MAY 1980
Aberdeen University.

3 MAY 1980
Newcastle University.

4 MAY 1980
Valentinos, Edinburgh.

5 MAY 1980
Tiffanys, Edinburgh.

6 MAY 1980
Top Rank, Sheffield.

8 MAY 1980
Routes, Exeter.

9 MAY 1980
Digbeth Civic Hall, Birmingham.

10 MAY 1980
Liverpool University.

11 MAY 1980
Rainbow, London. Support is by The Passions, The Fall and The Au Pairs. Following this, the band head over to Europe for their first full continental tour.

25 MAY 1980
A late night swimming trip ends with the band and road crew being arrested for indecent exposure on a beach in Rotterdam.

31 MAY 1980
Herford, West Germany – and Simon's birthday. Robert improvises a version of 'Happy Birthday' over 'Three'.

5 JUNE 1980
A show at Lyons University is cancelled after the band get lost in the mountains on their way to the venue.

14 JUNE 1980
A French festival with The Clash, Kevin Coyne and UFO. A riot ensues and the police employ teargas to disperse the crowd. Following this, headliners Roxy Music decide not to play and the show ends abruptly, in chaos.

While in France, the band also perform one show for the benefit of French radio. A version of 'At Night', recorded at this show, later appears on 'Curiosity'.

19 JUNE 1980
Ruffles, Aberdeen.

20 JUNE 1980
George Street Theatre, Edinburgh.

JULY 1980
The band are invited to Holland for a string of outdoor concerts. One of these, at Venedaal, is recorded for radio broadcast. The band are also interviewed by Paul Morley, for the *NME*. Robert, the writer pronounces, is "always on a fine line between agitation and boredom, and such a balance turns out faintly, deviously charming. He's no pretentious mock-recluse, perpetually feigning intensity of vision. He's never quite sure what to say. He's never quite sure about those around him. Does he take himself seriously? 'I do take myself seriously, but there's a point beyond which you become a comic figure'." Later, Robert says, "I've always written things down, ever since I can remember. Mainly because sometimes I get angry. I've got a really violent temper but it's not physical because I don't think I should vent my frustrations and depressions on to anyone else. I don't throw tantrums or anything like that, so I go off somewhere rather than smash the room. I write things down. It's a release. But I haven't got over the idea of separating communicating from preaching, a failure in a sense. I worry that my words aren't going to interest people because they're mainly about me, how I feel, they're not about world situations and alternatives.

"I've got faith in what I'm doing from a personal point of view but as to whether I go down in history I'm very doubtful about that so I don't let it worry me. If I let that worry me I'd crack up before I'm going to anyway."

29/30 JULY 1980
Shows at Auckland's Mainstreet Cabaret introduce The Cure to a New Zealand audience for the first time.

AUGUST 1980
When the band arrived in Australia they had but seven shows scheduled. They end up playing 24, with barely three days' rest. Being pent up at such close quarters for so long unleashes many tensions, musical and personal, and on arriving back in England, Matthieu announces he is leaving the group, and the band is once again a trio. Simon tells *Sounds*, "If any one of us three left, The Cure would be no more."

Last night of the 1980 UK tour: Robert (left) and Simon (above) at London's Rainbow.

SEPTEMBER 1980
Rehearsals begin for the third Cure album, but with little success. Demos recorded at Morgan towards the end of the month are scrapped. The same month, 'Grinding Halt' is included on the soundtrack to the movie, *Times Square*.

OCTOBER 1980
Another European tour, 27 dates taking the band around Scandinavia, the Low Countries, France and Germany. Virtually every show sells out and '17 Seconds' reaches the Top 10 in Belgium and The Netherlands.

NOVEMBER 1980
With another British tour looming, the band ask for local bands to send in demo tapes so that they might have a different support act in every town. Only Universities open to the general public are included in the itinerary.

18 NOVEMBER 1980
Cardiff University. The Cure complete six months of touring around 13 countries.

18 DECEMBER 1980
The Cure celebrate Christmas early with an invitation-only show at Notre Dame Hall, London. The Banshees, The Associates, The Scars and Tarzan Five all play.

FEBRUARY 1981
Work begins on 'Faith', The Cure's third album, at Morgan Studios. Over the next month the sessions are to shift from here to first Red Bus studios, then The Roundhouse, then Trident and finally Abbey Road. At the same time, Robert is writing material for the record in churches. Amongst the new instruments employed on the recording are strings on 'Funeral Party' and flute on 'Other Voices'.

The album takes most of the month to complete, after which the band turn their attention to composing the soundtrack to a film, *Carnage Visors*, which Simon's brother, Rick, has made to replace support bands on The Cure's upcoming British tour. This soundtrack was recorded in one day at Point Studios.

Robert:"We went to a lot of people in the film schools and that, but there was no commitment. We were offering them the opportunity to make a film but they were very jaded. You think they'd be interested in making a film, in an opportunity to work in their medium. We were going to put up the money and as long as they worked within certain guidelines, a certain atmosphere, they could do what they wanted. But there was no real enthusiasm. They were very cool about it.

"There were lots of reasons for not having support bands. On the last tour we did we put a thing in the music papers saying any local bands that would like to play with us should send a tape in, and we would choose a local band from each town we played in. Some of them were really good and it worked well. But the trouble is, if we arrive late for a soundcheck or if something goes wrong we've got to make a choice – either the support band gets a soundcheck and you get half as long as you need, so your sound's awful and the audience is disappointed, and they may not even like the support band, or the support group doesn't get a soundcheck and you get a good one and the audience is pissed off all the way through the support act because they can't hear anything. And then we were worrying about why there should be such things as support groups anyway, and a main band, and how can you justify who is better than who."

Richard's first version of the film, "a film-film with people," as Robert describes it, is aborted when he realises he has the light settings wrong – and the film turns out almost completely black. "We thought he was going to hang himself when

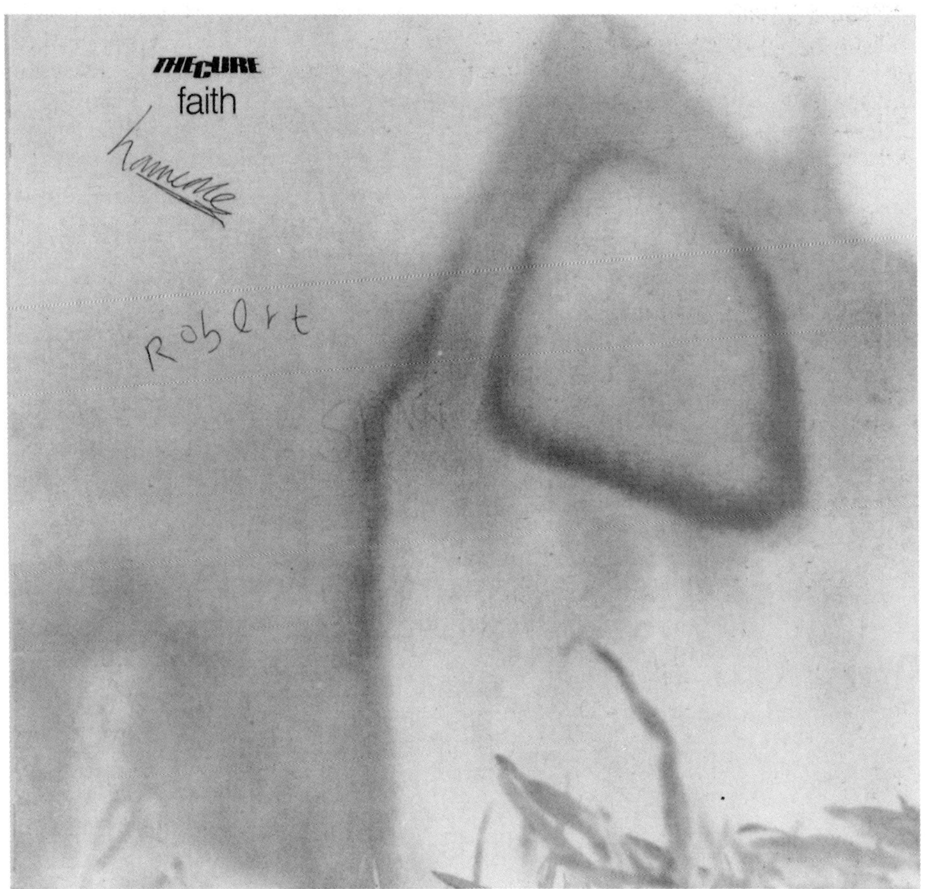

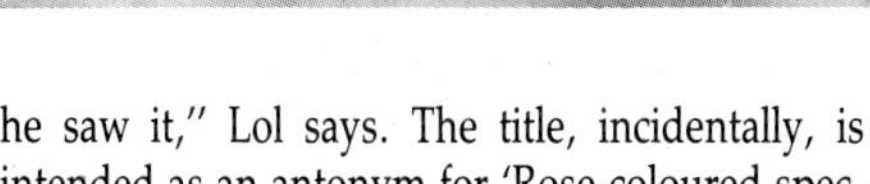

he saw it," Lol says. The title, incidentally, is intended as an antonym for 'Rose-coloured spectacles'.

"It's not very good, just a series of evolving shapes for people to look at while Smith's austere soundtrack further imposes the correct conditions of The Cure's entrance." (*NME*).

27 MARCH 1981

'Primary'/'Descent' is released as the band's next single. The picture sleeve was designed by Porl Thompson. A Top Of The Pops appearance swiftly follows, and the single eventually reaches number 43. This release marks The Cure's first 12" single.

11 APRIL 1981

'Faith' is released, its cover, a misty, grainy shot of picturesque Bolton Abbey near Shipton in North Yorkshire. 'Carnage Visors' appears as a bonus 'B-side' to the cassette version of the album. It was, Robert claims, originally intended "to be a very positive record. It turned into a very morbid record. There were just personal reasons which affected everyone at the time. We then had to live with it for a year, in that we toured with it – and it was the one record we shouldn't have done that with, because for one year we lived with this doomy, semi-religious record. We sort of wore it everywhere we went, it was like sack cloth and ashes. It wasn't a very enjoyable year really." Later, however, he says, "I've always tried to make records that are of one piece, that explain a certain kind of atmosphere to the fullest. If you're going to fully explore something you need more than one song to do it. That's why I always liked Nick Drake's albums, or Pink Floyd records like 'Ummagumma'. I like a lot of music which is built around repetition, Benedictine chants and Indian mantras. These musics are built around slow changes, they allow you to draw things out."

Unfortunately, reviews of the album are not complimentary. Elsewhere in *Record Mirror* the band are accused of being "stuck in the hackneyed doom mongering which should have died with Joy Division," with Mike Nichols writing, "Whereas PIL continue to radically rewrite their rule book, The Cure are lost in the maze of their spineless meanderings, hollow, shallow, pretentious, meaningless, self important and bereft of any real heart and soul." *NME* says, "In Sniffin' Glue's glory days they used to write happily of hurling records out of the window if they didn't come up to the exacting standards of the time. This one would have gone straight out, no messing about. Young English groups have created a whole new song-writing category known to experts as Grammar School Angst, and this collection represents a major contribution to the genre. It's very well played, beautifully recorded and says absolutely nothing meaningful in a fairly depressing way."

18 APRIL 1981

Friars, Aylesbury. The opening night of The Picture Tour. The band's PA has been hired from Pink Floyd. "After we hired the PA we had a day at Shepperton to see how it would look all set up. It

was really absurd seeing it all, 10 times larger than the equipment we usually use. But then we got to thinking we've always gone on tour with equipment breaking down. And at the moment it's reliability we want."

20 APRIL 1981
Arts Centre, Poole.

21 APRIL 1981
Guildhall, Portsmouth.

22 APRIL 1981
Top Rank, Brighton.

23 APRIL 1981
New Theatre, Oxford. "It happened two nights running. The Cure were about four numbers into their set. As they paused for breath between songs, yells went up round the hall – 'Forest', 'Primary', '10.15 Saturday Night'. We've paid our money and we want hits, dammit. Singer and guitarist Robert Smith stepped to the microphone and said, 'This one's called 'The Funeral Party'. I thought I saw a hint of a smile." (*Melody Maker*).

24 APRIL 1981
Brangwyn Hall, Swansea.

25 APRIL 1981
Odeon, Taunton.

26 APRIL 1981
Hexagon, Reading. "What the lack of a support band ensures is a total Cure diet without interruptions. In a way it sums up the current Cure direction. They allow a sense of doom and fatalism to hang over them with a sense of personal election. At times they seem more impressed by their own exclusive use of a doomy vocabulary than convinced of it, white ghouls taking glamour from their pallor. But at their best their religious devotional care and slow stately pace takes over with a precision and a discipline that is breathtaking and, yes, religious." (*NME*).

27 APRIL 1981
Odeon, Canterbury.

28 APRIL 1981
Gaumont, Ipswich.

29 APRIL 1981
Odeon, Chelmsford. "Cure concerts leave very little to chance. As soon as people enter the auditorium they're taken in hand by taped music guaranteed to create the right ambience. The music ranges from Jimi Hendrix to Gregorian chants – spot the importance of the latter to the likes of the gloomy 'Funeral Party'." (*NME*).

Of the older songs in the 'Faith' dominated set, Robert says, "I think it's nice remembering things. Having old songs is like having old photographs, you can look back on how you used to feel. I can remember what we felt the first time we played them, and that helps prevent me from getting out of control."

30 APRIL 1981
Civic Hall, Guildford.

1 MAY 1981
Polytechnic, Plymouth.

2 MAY 1981
Colston Hall, Bristol.

3 MAY 1981
Odeon, Birmingham.

4 MAY 1981
Odeon, Hammersmith. "The Cure simply create a mood, the lyrics comparing with the very worst sixth form poetry . . . To avoid monotony they vary the tone from intense to very intense, but while the latter is atmospheric and sombre, any idiot with a synthesizer and a smattering of Kafka can do the same. It's when the angst is added to a pop sensibility, the synth swapped for that hollow, twangy guitar that they excel. Then I can love The Cure." (*NME*).

6 MAY 1981
Assembly Rooms, Derby.

7 MAY 1981
Apollo, Manchester.

8 MAY 1981
Sheffield University.

9 MAY 1981
Leeds University.

10 MAY 1981
Royal Court, Liverpool.

11 MAY 1981
DeMontfort Hall, Leicester.

12 MAY 1981
St.Andrews Hall, Norwich.

14 MAY 1981
Tiffanys, Glasgow.

15 MAY 1981
Capitol, Aberdeen.

16 MAY 1981
Odeon, Edinburgh.

17 MAY 1981
City Hall, Newcastle.

18 MAY 1981
Town Hall, Middlesbrough.

22 MAY 1981
May Ball, Dublin College.

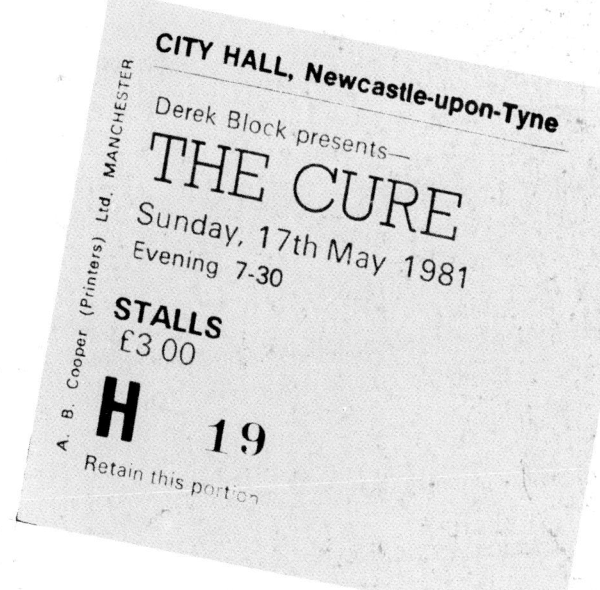

At the Werchter Festival in Belgium, July 1981.

JUNE 1981
The band return to Europe, touring first the conventional venues, then appearing in Holland with their own Big Top tent.

8 JUNE 1981
Stadthalle, Freiburg. No more than 40 people turn up for the show.

24 JUNE 1981
Lol's mother dies, news which reaches the band just before they take the stage at Sittard, in Holland. The band return to England the next day, and a tape of that concert is played at the funeral.

5 JULY 1981
Werchter, Belgium. Robert Palmer is on the same bill. At this show, The Cure stun onlookers with the 15-minute mogadon-pace version of 'A Forest', which closes their set.

16/17 JULY 1981
The band record their next single, 'Charlotte Sometimes'. They also make their latest video, in an abandoned psychiatric hospital. Former Supersonic director Mike Mansfield, now enjoying some success with Adam And The Ants, directs – a bizarre coupling, the results of which totally fail to impress the band.

23 JULY 1981
The Cure return to the US, opening the tour with two nights at the New York Ritz. From there they fly out to the west coast, playing shows in Pasadena, the LA Whiskey A-Go-Go and San Francisco. The Picture Tour then crossed the Pacific for New Zealand and Australia before doubling back on itself for a string of gigs in Canadian cowboy joints.

SEPTEMBER 1981
The band are given a fortnight's respite before setting off for a French tour, opening on 30 September. They reconvene as a trio, Matthieu Hartley having left at the end of the Australian tour. Robert doesn't seem too distressed. "It just means I have to do a lot more work now that the keyboards are gone, make more noise. I used to be able to get away with being a lazy sod on stage in the past." He adds, ". . . there isn't going to be anyone to fill that fourth position anyway. It would be impossible for someone else to fit into The Cure now because it's so popular it's untrue. It would take someone about 10 years to get accepted on the same level that we accept each other, and it's so open between the three of us, there are no regrets. It's like being married in a way. It's that same type of intensity you have to build on."

17 OCTOBER 1981
The French tour ends and the band return home, where 'Charlotte Sometimes'/'Splintered In Her Head' has been released as their latest single. It reaches number 44 in the chart. Simultaneously, copies of an American double album, entitled 'Happily Ever After' and consisting of the band's last two albums, begin filtering through the import racks.

21 NOVEMBER 1981
New Musical Express publishes a two page article, written by Paul Morley, under the impression that he is Robert Smith.

"You can wake up and think 'What the fuck am I doing in Canada? Why don't I go and live by the sea and work in a greengrocers?' If a Foster's can hits you, you know you're in Australia. When we visit all those countries we only see what we're allowed to see because of who we are and what we like. It still doesn't feel like I've seen much of the world. It's very rare that you dare go out alone. The only times I went out on my own I didn't come back. And I didn't remember where I'd been anyway."

25 NOVEMBER 1981
Lyceum, Sheffield. The Cure begin another British tour, supported by And Also The Trees and 1313, a duo comprising Steve Severin and Lydia Lunch. "Jo from And Also The Trees is nice isn't he? When the Trees came on tour with us, Jo used to do Mark E. Smith impersonations in the wardrobe because the echo was good. He was brilliant at it, and he knew all the words."

26 NOVEMBER 1981
Odeon, Edinburgh.

27 NOVEMBER 1981
Pavilion, Glasgow.

28 NOVEMBER 1981
St. George's Hall, Bradford.

29 NOVEMBER 1981
Kings Hall, Stoke.

30 NOVEMBER 1981
Apollo, Coventry.

1 DECEMBER 1981
Dome, Brighton.

3 DECEMBER 1981
Hammersmith Palais, London. The final night of the tour. Robert, Lol and Simon then move into a studio to begin working out ideas for the next album. The decision to abandon producer Mike Hedges, who had worked with them since '3 Imaginary Boys' is made easier when he is asked to produce the Banshees' next album, 'A Kiss In The Dreamhouse'. The Cure meanwhile opt to work with Phil Thornally, whose most recent clients include Duran Duran and the Thompson Twins.

JANUARY 1982
Work begins on the fourth Cure album.

6 MARCH 1982
New Musical Express reveal that the new Cure album is to be entitled 'Pornography', but quotes a Polydor spokesperson as remarking, "Whether or not it actually goes out under that title remains to be seen."

18 APRIL 1982
Skating Bowl, Plymouth. The first date of the Fourteen Explicit Moments Tour, supported by Zerra 1. While the band tour, 'Pornography' is released to mixed reviews. The most common accusation is that the album is 'violent', an accusation which Robert later refutes totally. "It wasn't really violent. It was the inability to be violent. It was a realisation of shortcomings – the fact that the music couldn't be violent enough to break out of those confines. I'd like to do something that is musically violent. Seventy-five per cent of The Cure's stuff I've been disappointed with. I've enjoyed much more than that while we're doing it, and revitalising it live. The live atmosphere has always been better."

"Phil Spector in Hell." (*NME*).

In another interview Robert says, "A lot of people have always had a very superficial idea of what we were like – imagining us as a grey, gloom band or whatever, but we have been quite diverse anyway . . . One of the problems is that people usually lump '17 Seconds', 'Faith' and 'Pornography' together, but they ARE all very different in sound and (lyrically) in subject matter. Apart from my voice, which is quite constant, 'Faith' and 'Pornography' are like two different groups."

Unfortunately the truth behind this remark is lost on the reviews, the general tone of which was just as Robert bemoaned: "another miserable album from that same old miserable band." 'Pornography' had a frenetic edge to it which the stately 'Faith' really approached only on 'Primary' and 'Doubt', and while it was never evident at the time, in retrospect the cracks which were to appear in the band's make-up over the next few months were already beginning to show.

"I hate the idea that you'd die for your audience. I was rapidly becoming enmeshed in that around the time of 'Pornography', the idea that Ian Curtis had gone first and I was soon to follow. I wasn't prepared for that to happen because I'm having too much fun."

19 APRIL 1982
Hexagon, Reading.

20 APRIL 1982
Colston Hall, Bristol.

21 APRIL 1982
Dome, Brighton. "Like any valid palliative, The Cure have not stood still inside the age that gave them birth. In these oppressive times they have made themselves grow equally fearsome. Three boys with very white knuckles and an awful lot on their minds . . . But then, what is Robert Smith singing about? I doubt if his listeners know and I'm not sure I do. It's easy to be obsessed by Smith in a live situation, stubbornly static and spellbound by his microphone, but it is the unity of The Cure that pinions the attention. This is a search for an electric music that bludgeons, hacks and stabs at the greyness The Cure have always had cast over them . . . By the time they reach Hammersmith there'll be few groups this live or this powerful." (*NME*).

"Robert Smith seems to be paying the price for his heavy boozing these days. He's getting quite chubby. Better stick to your favourite Peruvian snuff, Rob – at least there's no calories in it." (*Record Mirror*).

22 APRIL 1982
Gaumont, Southampton.

23 APRIL 1982
Sheffield Polytechnic.

24 APRIL 1982
City Hall, Newcastle.

Backstage in Berlin, May 1982.

25 APRIL 1982
Pavilion, Glasgow.

26 APRIL 1982
Playhouse, Edinburgh.

27 APRIL 1982
Apollo, Manchester.

28 APRIL 1982
Odeon, Birmingham.

29 APRIL 1982
University of East Anglia, Norwich.

30 APRIL 1982
Leicester University.

1 MAY 1982
Hammersmith Odeon, London. The last date of the British tour. The band then head over to the continent for a month.

27 MAY 1982
Strasbourg. After the show a fight between Robert and Simon results in them both walking out of the band. Lol stayed behind, having ascertained that Robert, at least, would eventually return to the fold.

4 JUNE 1982
Robert – and Simon – return in time for the scheduled show at Aix en Provence.

11 JUNE 1982
Brussels, Ancien Belgique. The last date of the Pornography European Tour. Simon leaves the band immediately after.

"There's a lot of things I'd rather do than trek around countries being drunk and playing to drunk people. The tour was like a rerun of the worst movie you've ever seen. It's as if you're leaning against a wall, eyes closed, and when you come to you're in the same place you were a year before.

"We were cracking up so the people offstage began to crack up as well. Twenty-three people reverting to primitives is not a pretty sight. We were more like a rugby tour than a Cure tour."

JULY 1982
'Hanging Garden', from 'Pornography' is released as a single, and reaches number 34. Besides the regular 7" and 12" releases, the single also appears as a four-track double pack, backed by a selection of older songs recorded live during the tour. The band, however, are not around to celebrate its success. After visiting the recording studio where the Banshees are recording their 'Kiss In The Dreamhouse' album, Robert goes camping in Wales with Mary. Lol sets off for a month's holiday in Europe. Neither leaves a forwarding address, and Robert later admits that during this period The Cure have effectively dissolved.

"I despaired about the whole business, being in a band, being involved in the music bit. After a while it takes you over and you can't see out of it. It's important to me to have a sense of myself as a person outside of all of this, a sense of myself as a person and not just a member of a group."

During this lay-off, Lol switches from drums to keyboards. "We never let ourselves become jaded in our attitude. We always make changes if the excitement is no longer there. In The Cure there was room to develop myself in certain ways as a drummer, but after 'Pornography' perhaps I had exhausted most of the possibilities within that format."

London's Rainbow, May 1980.

Facing page: Socialising at the Camden Palace; Robert with Budgie (top), Siouxsie (centre) and Severin (bottom).

AUGUST 1982

Robert's dissatisfaction with The Cure shows through publicly when the magazine, *Flexi-Pop*, asks The Cure to record a song for them. The resultant 'Lament', written by Robert whilst he was away, is recorded by Robert and Steve Severin alone.

OCTOBER 1982

Meanwhile, Chris Parry has sensed the dissent in the band's ranks, the dissatisfaction with the way things are going, and calls Robert and Lol together to ask them to record a new single which will go completely against the grain, and explode whichever myths have since grown up around the band. With drummer Steve Goulding, late of Wreckless Eric's band, making up the numbers, the result is 'Let's Go To Bed'.

The next step is to make a video in a similar vein. Chris Parry contacts Tim Pope, currently enjoying some success as Soft Cell's director, a relationship which has endured until today.

"'Let's Go To Bed' would be on the raunchy side were it not for the video that goes with it . . . very tasteful." (*Video World*).

'Let's Go To Bed' is an immediate Top 50 hit, reaching number 44. But Robert is not 100 per cent happy. "I don't think it's a Cure song," he tells *Record Mirror*, and admits he originally wanted it released under a totally different name. "It's not that Cure songs are a formula, but they do have a central core. This single has been released to get daytime airplay and it's disappointing to me because it's the first time we've ever been seen to be involved in current trends or fashions. There are probably only a few thousand people who've held us up as examples to themselves, but if I were one of them I'd feel let down. For us to be seen bothering in an area I don't respect upsets me."

Later he claims, "If we ever have a number one record I'll disband the group immediately. I'd never let us be seen to be competing to be a number one group. It's all such nonsense."

He tells *New Musical Express*, "'Let's Go To Bed' was like going to a party. We made a record instead of getting drunk." And informs *Melody Maker*, "It was supposed to be a solo single so that I just took the blame for it. It wasn't commercial anyway. I realised when I did it – which is why I lost interest in it – that it wasn't horrible enough, it just wasn't quite dumb enough to be commercial, it didn't get anywhere, it didn't even get played on the radio."

NOVEMBER 1982

John McGeoch, who joined the Banshees after Robert returned to The Cure, leaves the band and Robert is drafted in as replacement again. While he is away, touring first Britain, then the continent, Lol kills time by producing an album for And Also The Trees.

Robert's stint in the Banshees, hardly surprisingly, confuses outside observers, and rumours fly that The Cure have finally broken up. Matters are not helped when Robert tells *Record Mirror*, "Talking about [The Cure] now is like going back to an old toy or game whose rules you've forgotten. I don't despair about losing touch with The Cure. It's more despairing to realise I'll never reach the heights of a Bach or Prokofiev."

18 DECEMBER 1982

Robert asks *Melody Maker*, "Do The Cure really exist any more? I've been pondering that question myself. See, as I wrote 90 per cent of the 'Pornography' album I couldn't really leave because it wouldn't have been The Cure without me. But it has got to a point where I really don't fancy working in that format again. Being involved, for four years, I was getting really sick of being surrounded by the same people all the time. I just felt really stale so I took a break and in that sense The Cure doesn't exist really. But I mean the name's still there – though to me, that's unimportant.

"People keep saying 'You mustn't break up', because it's become like an institution. That almost gives me an incentive to pack it in anyway. I think it's really awful seeing bands disintegrate slowly, in a stupid way, don't you?"

In perhaps his most revealing interview yet, he tells writer Steve Sutherland, "I've always aspired to be like the way certain bands affected me – Joy Division, New Order, The Banshees, Echo And The Bunnymen, that's a very few – but I think they've kept a sort of intensity.

"That's what I was always striving for with The Cure, but there were far too many things working against it really; things of our own making like the anti-image and all that rubbish. Instead of trying to get rid of that at an early stage, we flirted with it so there was nothing to latch on to. I realise now that was probably a big mistake, not establishing ourselves as personalities earlier on.

"But it wasn't through choice, it was through apathy more than anything else. It wasn't a conscious decision to nurture that image, it was apathy in the sense of not trying to adopt another. All that side of things never really bothered me because the criterion that was involved in what we did always came from me – as long as I would have bought the stuff we were producing, then that was enough reason for releasing the records."

Some months later Lol says, "I never thought The Cure would pack up because there's too much of a bond between me and Robert ever to let it fade away. There's loads of times when we've said 'We don't want to see each other for this length of time' or 'We can't do this, we can't do that', but in the end there's always something that brings us back. It's like a shared history, the fact that we remember all the things we've done together before and it triggers off something. Maybe it's like a recall of people's emotions."

All pics except above: 'The Love Cats'–"The song was originally a fantasy idea of a cat having kittens and you then put them all in a sack and throw them in a lake. But it got mutated."

JANUARY/FEBRUARY 1983

The Banshees tour moves on to Australia, New Zealand and Japan. While there, Robert tells a journalist, "I get on very well with Siouxsie, which is quite strange because I'm one of the few people who do. I think it's because I don't take her seriously, and it's novel for her to have someone to tell her to shut up because most people are too scared."

Of his role in the Banshees, he says, "I'm just there. I'm just the guitarist with the Banshees. There's nothing formal, which is probably why it's working. They get a bit fed up with me doing other things. My attitude to the Banshees is more fragmented than theirs. I beat them at pool. They get ratty." He and Siouxsie, he says, "have a cartoony relationship. We adopt different personas in different situations, like Batman and Robin. She'd probably say I'm more like The Penguin."

MARCH 1983

Robert returns to London with the Banshees, and is approached by Royal Ballet choreographer Nicholas Dixon to score 'Les Enfants Terrible'. Robert suggests they first try working on a lesser project, choreographing 'Siamese Twins' (from the 'Pornography' album) for the BBC TV programme Riverside. With Lol on keyboards Steve Severin on bass and Marc Almond's Venomettes on backing vocals, the song is performed live and greeted with considerable critical acclaim. Neither Robert nor Dixon are fully satisfied, however, and the ballet is put on ice.

Immediately after this, Robert and Steve Severin begin work on what they describe as a psychedelic pastiche, The Glove (named after a character in The Beatles' *Yellow Submarine* movie). The idea has been on their minds for several years, delayed only by commitments to either The Cure or the Banshees. But with both bands now on ice, and fellow Banshees Siouxsie and Budgie already moonlighting as The Creatures, Severin and Robert head into Britannia Row studios to work. Budgie's girlfriend, Zoo dancer and one time choreographer to Darts, Jeanette Landray, comes in as vocalist.

Says Jeanette, "Basically because it was so clearly Robert and Steve's project I had a strange role, involved but not with any say in the way things turned out, almost like a session musician really. I don't know what I'd actually expected but if I was offered something similar again I'd have a much clearer idea of the problems involved. I'm not bitter about it but I have had to fight to get this far and it did get me some very useful exposure but I just under-estimated how little expression I'd have in the promotion of the album. I still feel like a faceless voice to some extent. It's very much Steve's and Robert's baby though but that was always clear so I can't complain."

Originally the project was going to end with a one-off single. "But when we went into the studio we ended up with 15 songs after three days. And we put them on a record. An odd record. It's an anachronism. No, it's Severin's answer to The Creatures. Actually, we had the idea around the time of 'Faith'. But it's turned out completely different to how we imagined. It's a real summer album, all songs and lots of funny instruments like kotos and dulcimers." Of Jeanette's contributions, Robert admits, "She'd never really sung before. In some of it she sings really well but in other bits . . . She didn't have enough time to work on the songs, I think. Like she was originally really shocked by lines like, 'Fuck me to death' and wasn't too happy about doing them."

The project is fuelled by endless horror/B-movies, consumed by Robert and Steven between sessions. "It was a real attack on the senses," Robert says later. "We were virtually coming out of the studio at six in the morning, watching all these really mental films and then going to sleep and having these really demented dreams. Then, as soon as we woke up, we'd go straight back into the studio, so it was a bit like a mental assault course by the end. We must have watched about 600 videos at the time! There'd be like all these after-images of the films we'd watched cropping up in the songs. It sounded like 15 different groups, like a K-Tel compilation album.

"The other thing that influenced us was the amount of junk we were reading, the amount we spent on idiot magazines. We were making big murals of all these cuttings and pictures and stuff, big Day-Glo posters."

At the same time, it is important that the album should be enjoyable. Robert tells *International Musician*, "We didn't want it to sound like a self-indulgent album made by two ageing hippies."

He adds in an interview with *Smash Hits*, "Severin brings out the lighter side of my character because he's pretty grumpy, so I compensate by being unnaturally chirpy. Whereas with Lol a cynical lethargy creeps in because I tend to rely on him for entertainment. I think he (Lol) is suffering from a massive personality disorder due to oppressed beastliness. But basically he's quite nice."

And finally, Robert tells *Flexi-Pop*, "I need a holiday. I keep making plans to go every week, but every week I'm in another group!"

12 MARCH 1983

Melody Maker announces that "Simon Gallup, the bass player who recently parted company with The Cure, has joined forces with another ex-Cure man to form a new group called Cry. Besides Gallup and keyboard player Matthieu Hartley, the band also features Stuart Curran, Ian Fuller and the concisely named Tot." The band later change their name when confronted with another group called Cry, and become Fools Dance.

APRIL 1983

The Cure are offered a headlining role on BBC TV's Oxford Road Show. It is suggested they perform 'Let's Go To Bed' and 'Just One Kiss'; Robert decides 'Figurehead' and '100 Years' would be better. With Andy Anderson, drummer with Brilliant, and SPK pianist Derek Thompson, Robert and Lol put in a performance which finally wipes away any doubts they may have had regarding the future of The Cure.

"It was fun because we actually played live. Also, it was great being on the same programme as Kajagoogoo."

Almost immediately, work begins on a new single, 'The Walk'.

JULY 1983

'The Walk'/'Upstairs Room' is released and becomes an instant, and massive, hit, peaking at number 12. Robert says, "It's nice that it's got into the charts for the sole reason that it'll be heard on the radio. I'm not being big headed but I think it's better than 90 per cent of what you hear on the radio now.

"I didn't expect it to get so high, but I'd suspected something was up when my mum liked it. She normally hates any Cure stuff I play her.

"It's difficult to explain what's important, but I'd rather listen to 'One Hundred Years' than 'The Walk'. I still prefer albums to singles. All the singles we've done are just odd things we've thought of, dumb singles . . . That's all we've done since 'Pornography', dumb singles."

He also confesses, "We knew that 'The Walk' would be compared to 'Blue Monday' (New Order's seminal hit, released around the same time) but it would have been wrong not to have released it because of that."

Later he says, "I'm surprised that 10 times the number of people bought 'The Walk' than did 'Charlotte Sometimes', but I don't worry about it. They're not released to compete." Dutch fans are offered a six-track mini album, 'The Walk', containing tracks from both the UK 'The Walk' 12" single and its predecessor.

The band make two Top Of The Pops appearances in aid of 'The Walk' – a video had been made, with Tim Pope again at the helm, but the BBC veto it. Apparently they are worried by the sight of the band members in make-up, a disguise which Robert and Lol changed for every take. Together with Andy Anderson, Porl Thompson appears on the first TOTP performance, Phil Thornally on the second.

Thornally is best known for his work as engineer with the likes of The Psychedelic Furs, Paul McCartney, Duran Duran and Thompson Twins. "He fancied a bit of culture for a change," Robert claims.

"I think I must be a bit hyper-active or something," responds Thornally.

"The Cure on TOTP was an event almost as absurd as Jimmy Savile's inanity. They looked and acted bored, but all across the nation Cure fans, Cure converts and folk who can't tell The Cure from Culture Club and couldn't care less, interpreted Smith's stifled yawns as enigmatic arrogance. Such is the power of reputation, such is the impact of dressing in black." (*Melody Maker*).

Robert also appears on Riverside with The Glove around this time, performing 'Punish Me With Kisses'.

A first for the group: Robert and 'dancing' Lol in the video for 'The Walk', during which their make-up changed on every take.

The Glove, conceived originally for a one-off single but . . . "We ended up recording 15 songs in three days and we put them on a record."

AUGUST 1983

The Cure – Robert, Lol, Andy and Phil – headline the Elephant Fayre at St. Germains, Cornwall. They warm up for the show with two low-key gigs in Bath and Bournemouth.

"People came up after we played and said, 'Oh it was really enjoyable,' but we didn't want it to be. It was so nostalgic, all those songs we played. Somehow I feel I've compromised it, this big leap between 'Pornography' and what we do next, by allowing us to play live. I've recognised the history of the Cure again.

"It was simply entertainment . . . Admittedly there wasn't the same power as before but that would have been impossible. I can't imagine being involved in anything as intense as the Pornography Tour ever again. We definitely are not concerned with striving to recapture past glories. It is completely different with Phil and Andy from how it was with Simon in the group."

"Robert Smith raises fourth form poetry to new heights. Here are some of the key words without which a Cure song would cease to exist: 'mouth', 'finger', 'eye', 'cold', 'kiss', 'mirror', 'die', 'cry' and most important of all, 'I'." (*NME*).

After the Fayre, the band head off for a short tour of America.

Lol says, "It was funny there, because 50 per cent of the audience were the sort of people I'd have expected to turn up, people who'd bought our albums etc. But the other 50 per cent were people who'd seen 'Let's Go To Bed' on MTV. There were 14-year-old schoolgirls screaming, which was funny."

He continues, "Real Beatlemania. It got a bit absurd towards the end. I'd never thought I'd see the day when you'd get a bra thrown up on stage at a Cure gig; I just laughed myself stupid about it."

Returning to Europe, the band make their way to Paris where they are booked into the Studio Des Dames. There they record the most atypical Cure single yet, 'Love Cats'.

"That song fulfilled an idea to put out an amateurish pop song rather than do an obvious follow-up to 'The Walk'. A year and a half ago we wouldn't have released something like that because it wouldn't have fitted in with the idea of The Cure. The area we work in now is much looser and we have the freedom to release one-off singles like that."

This same month, The Glove's 'Like An Animal' single is also released.

SEPTEMBER 1983

Robert travels to Italy with the Banshees, for a gig in Rome and a video shoot in Venice. A rehash of The Beatles' 'Dear Prudence', the Banshees' latest single, is Robert's first recording with the band. "Whatever next," ponders the *NME*, "'Bungalow Bill'?" The entourage then moves on to Israel where they are scheduled to tour.

In between social events, Robert begins work on the next Cure album, whilst back at home, The Glove's 'Blue Sunshine' album is released.

"I think 'Blue Sunshine' was very much a summer album which was why we called it that. All those instruments like kotos and dulcimers are very summery in feel and yes, I suppose 'Blue Sunshine' will remain as some sort of souvenir of that long, hot summer. Yes, of course it was very indulgent, which is why so few people here bought it. But overall it sold quite well round the world. In some of the oddest places!"

30 SEPTEMBER/1 OCTOBER 1983

The Banshees headline London's Royal Albert Hall, concerts which are both televised and recorded for a forthcoming double album, 'Nocturne'. Robert admits, "A lot of the time I'm still trying to play John McGeoch's guitar parts and failing. If I went on like this for a few more months I'd be the next one to have a breakdown. It's fine at the moment, though. It's a balancing act and as long as I don't fall over it'll be all right."

Nevertheless, 'Nocturne' comes in for a hard time with the music press. "Many critics felt it to be the ultimate repudiation of all that punk had stood for, and the idea of any punk band, let alone one described by the *NME* as '1978's most subversively stimulating band' – wheeling out such an old wave warhorse as a double live album was enough to induce apoplexy." (*Record Collector*).

25 OCTOBER 1983

'Love Cats'/'Speak My Language' is released, the last in what Robert describes as The Cure's Fantasy trilogy and the most successful yet – it reaches number seven. "From now on we'll be heading back into the abyss. If 'Pornography' took you to the edge of the cliff, the next one will plunge you over it.

"I've always found it difficult to write 'up' songs. 'Love Cats' was just a phrase, like banana-fish, just a fantasy idea of a cat having kittens and you put them all in a sack and you throw them all in a lake. And it just got mutated. It was originally something I read in a Patrick White novel, 'The Cockatoos', and it said 'His cat had become pregnant by an unknown tomcat and so its kittens were known as the love cats.' The book said, as soon as they were born . . . 'we put the love cats in a sack and threw them in the lake.' That line was originally the start of the song's chorus. But when we were doing it I thought I can't really sing this."

Later he admits that cats do appeal to him, simply because "They seem to do very little except make little funny noises, fuck, eat and sleep."

Elsewhere he confesses, "I've had people write to me that we've sold out but I don't see that at all. "We've done 'Love Cats' to stop people categorising us. This year we decided that we'd take a break from touring and we'd just do three singles that are all quite different from each other. They're just experiments more than anything else, just songs we had that were fun to do." And apart from those singles, "which were experimental, we don't make records unless we have a wealth of experience to write about. It's got to feel worthwhile. At the moment we're storing them up to do another album.

"If we purely did things like 'The Love Cats' I'd hang myself."

The video sees the band transported to a room alive with cats, although according to Lol, "The funniest thing about making the video was the woman who looked after the cats. She looked more like a cat than any of her animals did. We had about 30 cats altogether and they wouldn't do anything we wanted them to. There was loads of cat food in strategic places to encourage them into the shot, but they hated the stuffed cats and they all ran away when we let them into the room."

"Arguably their best single to date, the swinging 'Love Cats' . . . " (*International Musician*).

NOVEMBER 1983

On Top Of The Pops, Robert forgets the words to 'Love Cats', but the single goes on to make number seven regardless. A second Glove single, 'Punish Me With Kisses', however, flops. As for The Glove's future plans, Robert says, "There's been talk of us doing a 'Music For Dreams' album. A pure instrumental, but that's way in the future. It's just something we talk about in a drunken state."

'The Love Cats' video.

Right: In Between Daze.

Below: Robert, during the filming of 'In Between Days'.

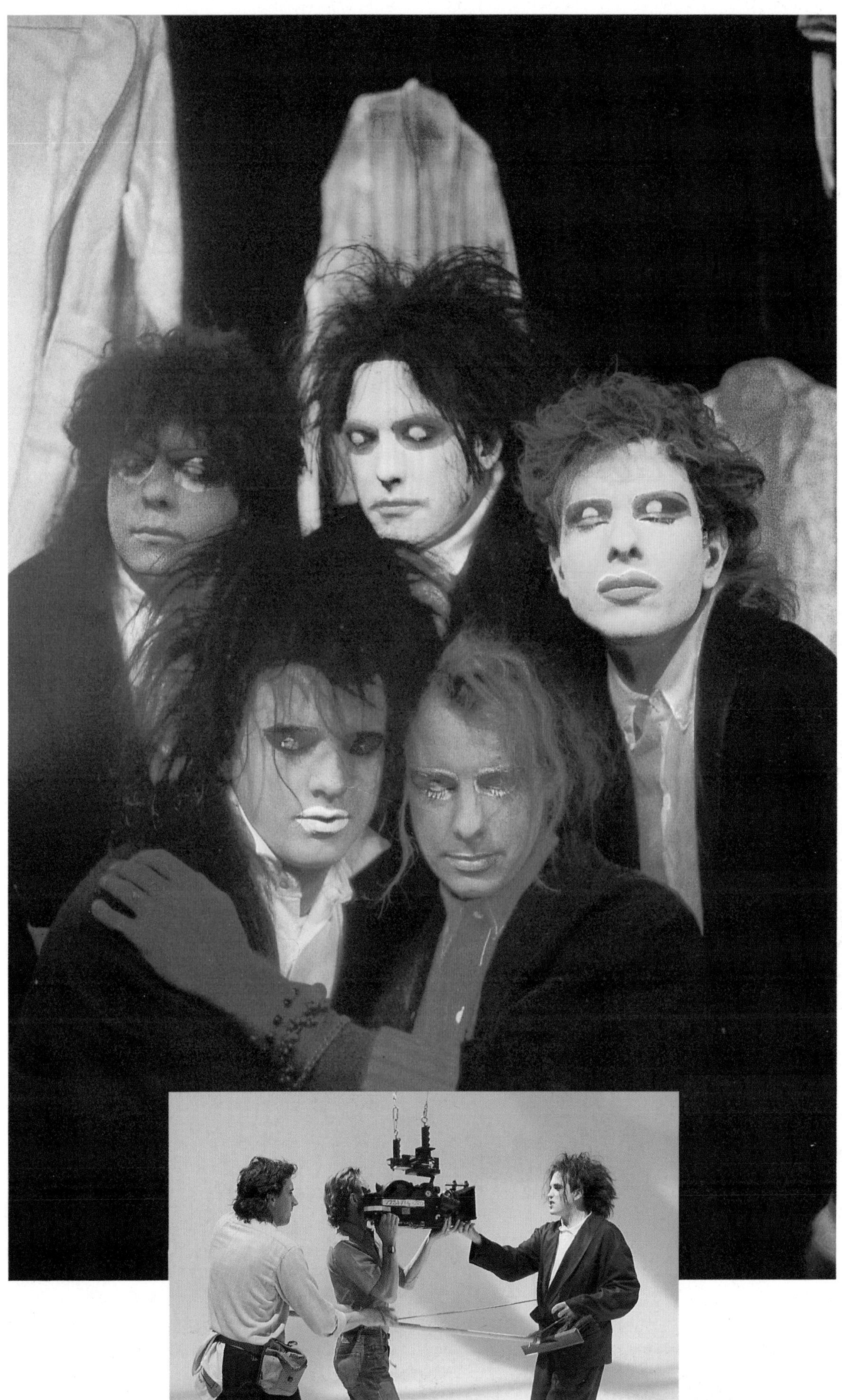

DECEMBER 1983

'Japanese Whispers', an eight-track compilation of the last three singles and their B-sides is released. Originally targeted solely at the Japanese and German markets, it is given a full British release and prompts *Sounds'* Bill Black to warn, "Beware! All the signs are that Smith intends to return to the plodding ground of past work for the next album, so get happy while you can."

Smith responds, "I think it'll be really odd when we do something serious. People will think it's really morbid and they'll go, 'Oh, this is a bit of a change for The Cure, I always thought they were a pop group'."

18 DECEMBER 1983

Record Mirror asks Robert what annoys him about other groups. "I always think it's really funny when those totally manufactured groups like Duran Duran arrive in a blaze of glamour, and when they've made lots of money they want to be taken as Serious Artists. And like Adam Ant returns with his 'new image' and he's got a different coloured frilly shirt on. I used to go into whole evening discussions on how to mutilate certain people but I've become much more tolerant now."

25 DECEMBER 1983

Robert appears on Top Of The Pops with both the Banshees ('Dear Prudence') and The Cure ('Love Cats'), both bands celebrating their biggest hits yet.

"We don't smile enough to fit in [on TOTP]. I find it really hard to pretend to see through that camera into the homes of those millions of people who are really going to love you. It's such a farce. I look really bored because I am. We only do it because if we didn't someone else would."

JANUARY 1984

Robert opens the new year dividing his time equally between the Banshees' new album, 'Hyaena', and The Cure's 'The Top'. He also found time to work with Tim Pope on the latter's single, 'I Want To Be A Tree'.

Neither album session went smoothly. The Banshees' set in particular had dragged on and on, primarily because of Robert's commitments with The Cure. Indeed, he was even absent from the final mix, with Steve Severin complaining, "He's off making another space opera with The Cure . . . [which is] a pity because he's really good in the studio and it's always useful to have another pair of ears."

'The Top', on the other hand, suffered because bassist Phil Thornally was in Australia, working as engineer on Duran Duran's latest album, 'Seven And The Ragged Tiger'. Robert filled the breach himself.

The Pope single, on the other hand, goes like a dream. Says Pope, "I had to make a showreel of my films so I decided to go right over the top and do an hour and a half, really pretentious job, just to get all these ideas out of my system. I wanted to end it with something really stupid, so there was this song lying around which a friend and I had written when I was 18. We recorded it over Christmas, then I called up various people who I'd worked with and who were in London at the time. It was all a huge joke, but within seven days of the showreel going out I'd been offered seven record deals."

MARCH 1984
The Banshees release their 'Swimming Horses' single. To promote it, the Banshees – with Robert again on guitar – tour. At the same time, Siouxsie remarks, "Fat Boy Smith is nothing to do with the new album except that he actually plays on it."

"To be perfectly straight, as far as Siouxsie is concerned I'm just the guitarist with her band. There's nothing formal which might explain why it seems to be working out so successfully. I suppose they get fed up with me doing other things and having to arrange their schedule to suit mine, but at least we have the same things in common, in that we're against six, seven, eight-week or even longer tours."

Elsewhere, Robert says, "I've had to rearrange my guitar sound so it sounds almost unlike me. I also play piano, organ and even sitars, a real pot-pourri. There's some strange non-instruments on it as well, like we've spun a coin, miked it up and slowed it down 20 times so it sounds like a merry-go-round. It took a whole day to record and we ended up not using it."

He later admits, however, he is not over-happy with the album. "After The Glove and playing about with the psychedelia thing it was time the Banshees got raw again and I thought that was the way it would go. It shouldn't have been 'Kiss In The Dreamhouse' part two. Lots of stuff came from me and Severin just staying up all night, playing and recording this and that, really rough and very powerful. But then the production smoothed it all out.

"I'm as much a member as I could be, but I don't have as much say as them. That's why it's always good when I go back to The Cure. I am The Cure."

While he awaits Robert's return, Lol produces Baroque Bordello's 'Today' and And Also The Trees' 'The Secret See'. "It's good that we do different things," he says. "I'm gonna do a solo single soon, with a couple of friends of mine. More than destroying things, it keeps us together. It's a fresher approach every time."

3 MARCH 1984
The Cure's latest tour dates announced in the British music press. The queues for tickets begin forming almost immediately.

24 MARCH 1984
Announced that a third night at Hammersmith Odeon has been added to the tour.

30 MARCH 1984
'The Caterpillar'/'Happy The Man' is released as The Cure's latest single. Robert, opines the *NME*'s Julie Burchill, is now sitting, "charmingly cross-legged, in the garden of English eccentricity." Tim Pope's video, meanwhile, plants the band in a greenhouse where, in a vague rerun of the 'Love Cats' film, both band and instruments are coated in caterpillars. The band also make another 'controversial' appearance on Top Of The Pops, this time sitting cross-legged on the stage. "We were knackered. We'd been in the studio all night and, I mean, why should we stand? Next time I may go on in bed."

Of the band's increasingly esoteric choice of material Robert says, "Over the four years The Cure have worked with Fiction and Polydor, they've realised that the more they pressure us to do something the less likely it is that it'll get done. They've learned to tolerate me like an awkward but inexpensive half-wit in the corner. The fact that we've never been in debt to a record company has allowed us a great deal more freedom than most bands. I've never seen The Cure as a career. It can't progress consciously – it could just as easily stop as keep going for years. It doesn't worry me. I don't plan. At the moment I'm involved in so many things because I get sick of being tied down to one area, to one set-up. The only disadvantage of doing so much is that it's not allowing me as much free time as I used to have to do things away from music. It's difficult to disappear – I haven't had a day off for about three months now and it's really getting to me."

APRIL 1984
The Cure appear on the Oxford Road Show as a prelude to their latest tour. Meanwhile, Glove vocalist Jeanette Landray tells *ZigZag*, "The Glove as a project is now virtually over; there may be odd bits and pieces here and there but I'm really concentrating on my own plans now . . . "

21 APRIL 1984
Record Mirror asks Robert what he would do if he were Prime Minister. "Review, rearrange, replace and rewrite the British political, legal, social and economic structures and systems."

26 APRIL 1984
Edinburgh Playhouse. The Cure launch onto their latest British tour. Robert: "Andy the drummer I got quite by accident – someone introduced us and even though our musical backgrounds were very different we just got on very well. He's probably technically the most competent out of us all. And Phil the bass player engineered 'Pornography' and that's how we met him, and he just fancied playing bass as he gets fed up just working in the studio. And Porl was in the original line up of the group seven years ago and he's been living with my sister ever since, and he does the artwork for the albums and singles. And Lol's still just there – I can't seem to shake him off."

"Flicka flicka flicka flicka . . . and they were gone." (*Sounds*).

27 APRIL 1984
Apollo, Glasgow.

29 APRIL 1984
Odeon, Birmingham.

30 APRIL 1984
Royal Concert Hall, Nottingham.

MAY 1984
The Banshees release their next single, 'Dazzle', a lushly produced epic which *Smash Hits* describes as, "An absolutely titanic meeting of the Onedin Line and a sixties wall of sound," and Robert claims "sounded like The Glitter Band or Sweet or something, really raw. And then they got in the orchestra."

Midway through The Cure's own tour, 'The Top' is released to excited reviews.

"Writing ['The Top'] was like starting again, like writing '3 Imaginary Boys'. I did loads of stuff, lots of nonsense and worked from that. There was so much it might have gone anywhere."

The Cure

The Cure

Right: Andy Anderson, Lol, Phil Thornally and Robert.

Below: left to right – Boris Williams, Robert, Lol, Porl and Simon.

Far right, inset: Robert and girl-friend Mary Poole.

Robert warns his fans, "People who have picked up on us through our last few singles will be shocked if they rush out to buy the album." Asked if this wasn't a little unfair, he replies, "That's just our way of having a bit of fun." Later, however, he admits, "'The Top' was so fucking deranged I thought people would start to get the wrong idea about me if I continued to write things like that."

Besides playing all the instruments bar drums, Robert also claims the album marks his début as a singer. "I was a bit of a whiner. The new songs would have sounded stupid if I'd whined them so I had to try and sing. My voice is better now than it was, but it's still a struggle to make it sound at all different. When I was singing on 'Caterpillar' I was worried I was going too far over the top."

In another interview, with *International Musician*, Robert admits, "I think subconsciously I made the decision to make 'The Top' different (from our other albums). It does resemble our first LP more than anything else we've done inasmuch as there is a variety of moods and styles. But although it's similar to '3 Imaginary Boys' in its diversity, the content is very different.

"It's funny. With the exception of the recent LP I've probably been disappointed with 75 per cent of The Cure's material, yet playing it on stage seems to thoroughly revitalise it. The live atmosphere has always been better with them (The Cure) while with Siouxsie there's a different power altogether."

He tells *Sounds*, "I could write more facile songs . . . like, the rest of the group have heard my 'singles' tape, most of which Nik Kershaw would die for – no, he's a serious artist now, say A-Ha – but they're dreadful, with really crass choruses. I've thought of releasing them under a pseudonym but I don't want people . . . you could write a shopping list but you don't want to be best known for your shopping lists."

"Either Smith's gone mad or we have . . . " (*Melody Maker*).

1 MAY 1984
Royal Court Theatre, Liverpool.

2 MAY 1984
Apollo, Manchester.

4 MAY 1984
Colston Hall, Bristol.

5 MAY 1984
Apollo, Oxford. Four tracks from the show – 'Shake Dog Shake', 'Primary', 'Charlotte Sometimes' and 'Give It Me' – eventually appear on The Cure's forthcoming live album, 'Concert'.

6 MAY 1984
Guildhall, Portsmouth.

8-10 MAY 1984
London Hammersmith Odeon, the last nights of the tour. The remainder of the 'Concert' album – 'Hanging Garden', 'The Walk', '100 Years', 'A Forest', '10.15 Saturday Night' and 'Killing An Arab' – is recorded at these three shows.

"Hit albums, hit singles, The Cure are stars. Doomy in their delivery, exuberant in their reception, and a billion times as valid as Smith's part time hobby, they could become the biggest thing to hit rock in ages. Robert Smith very nearly is." (*ZigZag*).

13-31 MAY 1984
The Cure tour Europe, making their first visit to Italy.

18 MAY 1984
Nice.

26 MAY 1984
Hamburg. Robert phones Steve Severin and admits the workload is getting too much for him. He offers to help out on the Banshees' British tour, but asks to be excused the American outing. Later he flies home, cancelling two Cure dates.

Steve Severin says, "He's been on tour for three years . . . it seems like it, anyway. I get these postcards from all over the world with 'HELP' written on them." Robert's place in the Banshees is taken by John Carruthers of Clock DVA.

JUNE 1984
The Banshees' 'Hyaena' album is released. "The time I spent with the Banshees was good. People forget things like 'Dear Prudence' which did really well. At the time I thought I knew which direction the Banshees should have taken, but it was never really my place to know because it was really all about Siouxsie and Severin.

"The stuff we did live was absolutely brilliant, but the recorded stuff didn't really have the same definition, and maybe it was a mistake to make that record. A lot of it is good, but it's not cohesive enough to be great."

Elsewhere, in an interview with *NME*, Robert says his present state of mind is "Happy but very muddled. I don't think it'll last – I just think I'm going through a mid-life crisis. The point where I stop working in contemporary music, I think, becomes increasingly close. In fact it's very close. I just don't want to have bits falling off me in public. I don't want to do it in front of cameras."

On a less sober note, Robert is interviewed by *International Musician* about his collection of musical instruments, and in particular, his Fish guitar. "That's a 1961 Fender Jazzmaster, heavily customised. I often hang a dead fish from the end."

In the same magazine, Phil Thornally reveals touring with The Cure represented "virtually a 90 per cent cut in wages." But then Thornally confesses to a curious enjoyment of The Cure's company and the pleasure which both recording and playing live with them brings.

"The thing about The Cure, and Robert Smith in particular, is that they are so original. I came from a background where everybody tried to be so technically perfect in their playing. It wasn't until I

ODEON HAMMERSMITH Tel. 01-748-4081
Manager: Philip Leivers
ADVANCE BOOKING TICKET
CONCERT
DATE
TIME
As advised at the time of purchase. (See reverse). Please see full seating plan on display
PRICE
CIRCLE
BLOCK
6
I X 9
NO TICKET EXCHANGED NOR MONEY REFUNDED
This portion to be retained
No re-admission

met people like Robert and Psychedelic Furs that I realised that originality is far more important. I actually have a record deal of my own, with Riva (Rod Stewart's label) and whenever I get the chance I try to put down things of my own. But compared with what Robert does, my stuff seems so worthless. You'd think it would be easy simply to be yourself, but I find I end up copying everybody else!"

25 AUGUST 1984

The Cure play Glasgow Barrowlands for the benefit of BBC TV's 'Rock Around The Clock' extravaganza. Robert spends the rest of the month playing through several days' worth of Cure tapes, selecting material to appear on 'Curiosity – Cure Anomalies, 1977-1984', the bonus B-side to the forthcoming 'Concert' live set. "I had so many tapes so I could listen to how we were going, and if anyone was making mistakes I'd go and visit them in their rooms in my Gestapo outfit and sort them out. There were certain things I thought would be fun for people to hear. I thought I'd pick out the best bits, put them on to one cassette and give the rest away – which I have done. Half of it is really good and half of it is . . . it's interesting if you like The Cure, but if you don't you'll be bored by it. Very bored. I listened to it the other day and some of it was terrible."

Tim Pope's 'I Want To Be A Tree' is released to favourable reviews, but low sales. The accompanying video, shown on Whistle Test shortly after the release of Tim's latest show reel, is sadly nowhere to be seen. Robert is evident throughout the single, Lol appears on the B-side, 'The Elephant Song'.

SEPTEMBER 1984

A feature in *Record Collector* magazine reveals that a complete Cure singles collection, purchased at current market rates, would cost in excess of £70. "To the collector . . . The Cure are as enigmatic as they are fascinating. Without ever resorting to gimmicks or quick sales incentives their back catalogue is littered with elusive cuts. And even when limited edition tactics have been employed, as with the 'Hanging Garden' double set or the three track 'Charlotte Sometimes' 12", the bonus pack is often worth only marginally more than the conventional release."

Right: In Belgium during the 1987 World Tour, left to right – Porl, Robert, Simon and Lol.

Below: In France.

POINT DEPOT
Port Átha Cliath
DUBLIN PORT
B+I

30 SEPTEMBER 1984
The next leg of The Cure World Tour opens in New Zealand. Over the next three months the band will visit Australia, Japan, Canada and the United States.

12 OCTOBER 1984
Sydney.

13 OCTOBER 1984
Leave Australia for Japan. Whilst in Tokyo, Robert sacks Andy because of the drummer's drinking problem. The band arrive in San Francisco without a drummer, but Phil sorts things out by contacting Vince Ely, one time Psychedelic Fur, who steps into the breach. He plays the next 11 shows before a prior engagement calls him back to the West Coast.

27 OCTOBER 1984
'Concert', The Cure's long-awaited live album, is released. Cassette versions feature the bonus 'Curiosity', comprising a collection of previously unreleased live cuts and demos.

"It's all been done very plainly. We only spent four days mixing it and it's not a very big budget number. It's a very trashy record, it doesn't glisten, it actually sounds like a concert."

NOVEMBER 1984
Chicago. Robert stops smoking. "I just decided that I should. I hate dependency on physical things and I didn't want to get to the stage where I had to have a cigarette. I can't remember ever wanting to give up drink, though. I think I've been drunk every night this year."

7 NOVEMBER 1984
Minneapolis. Thompson Twins' drummer Boris Williams' first gig with The Cure.

The Cure

Below: left to right – Porl, Boris, Robert, Simon and Lol.

FEBRUARY 1985

With Phil Thornally now entertaining visions of his own solo career, he quits The Cure and Simon Gallup, until now a member of Fools Dance, is invited back to the fold. The band now lines up as Robert, Lol, Simon, Porl and Boris.

MARCH 1985

The band go into the Angel Studios to begin work on their next album, 'The Head On The Door'. Robert reveals he has taken to staying up all night, and tells *ZigZag*, "I detest the bloke upstairs 'cause he plays the piano at six in the morning when I'm trying to get to sleep. Not only that, but he plays his own compositions. I don't do that to him, so I think it's really unfair. I've actually got into the very bad habit in the past three or four months of going to bed when it gets light and it's becoming really annoying. It's so bloody cold at night!"

APRIL 1985

Robert: "Steve Severin . . . I hate him. He slagged me off in some paper, so I invited him out tonight, and I'm going to beat him up."

JUNE 1985

The new five-piece Cure play together for the first time, in Barcelona. From here they go on to Italy. "When we go abroad we do try to retain a degree of culture and decorum even in our worst moments. We throw each other out of hotel windows rather than the furniture. A lot of the time I slag off the other bands that we play with, but it's something I quite enjoy, especially when we all glower at each other in the hotel foyer."

19 JULY 1985

'In Between Days'/'The Exploding Boy' is released as a single. It reaches number 15 in the chart. The accompanying video is a kaleidoscopic affair featuring an array of grotesquely coloured socks dancing around the band. "It all began when I said to the video director, Tim Pope, that we'd like flashes of colour going between my head when I was singing, and he said, 'What, colour like my socks?' and I said 'Yeah'. And that obviously stuck in his mind because socks are cheap and easy to come by. He tells us that he told the animators to use fluorescent socks in the colour scheme and they took him at his word. And they spent thousands of pounds drawing all those socks, frame by frame. Bloody mental! £8,000 – it's outrageous. Then it was all done and I got this anguished phone call apologising. At first I hated it, then I came round to it, but now I'm fed up with it because it's obliterated the idea of the video."

On the set for the video of 'In Between Days'. Tim Pope (pictured centre with his hand to his mouth) originally planned to have flashes of lurid colour moving around Robert as he sang. In the end there emerged a kaleidoscope of dancing socks. "At first I hated it," said Robert. "Then I came round to it but now I hate it again."

Also, the video was "exhausting, because I had to wear the camera strapped to me for five hours. What I hate about videos [is] having to be on call from first thing in the morning. If I had to go to Heaven at nine in the morning I think I'd be quite unhappy. You also have to put so much into them so it looks like you're having a good time when really you're in a semi-coma, wishing you were in bed."

27 JULY 1985

Antic Panathinaikos Stadium, Athens, sharing the bill with Nina Hagen, Talk Talk and Telephone. Robert: "I'm lucky because I'm quite short sighted so it doesn't matter if there's a thousand or 10 thousand people in the audience. I can't see further than the front row."

Boy George is also on the bill. He gets stoned off stage, but afterwards the staff of The Cure's hotel are convinced that Simon is *The* Boy, and insist on plying him with free champagne. Simon repays them with a chorus of 'Do You Really Want To Hurt Me'.

AUGUST 1985

'The Head In The Door' album is released. The title, Robert claims, dates from his childhood. "Did your mum and dad ever do puppet shows, like draw a face on their hands and go 'Waaargh!' from behind the sofa and really scare you? I've always been fascinated with puppets like Punch And Judy because the tradition is so old. There's something about the way a puppet's head will roll off. When they used to decapitate people they'd put their heads on poles and all your instincts just scream at that. So we were gonna call [the album] 'The Head On The Pole' and then I changed it."

Robert talks of recording an EP of Frank Sinatra songs, and admits, "If I wasn't in a band I'd start up The Cure right now because I still detest the people in the Top 10 as much as I did when we started.

"There's a lot of different songs but it's got the sort of continuity that those 'Disco Beach Party' albums have. There used to be a huge divide between people who liked the singles and the people who liked the albums, but with 'In Between Days' I think that divide's closed up because if you like that single, chances are you'll like the album as well.

"I prefer this record to 'The Top', it's a bit easier for me to like so I imagine it's easier for everybody else to like as well. Because I played all the instruments on 'The Top' except drums, it was easy to get carried away in a dense mixture of sounds but on this one, all five of us were there so there was a lot more communication of ideas. Eight of the songs are first takes which is something we haven't done since we made '17 Seconds' which, as everybody knows, was the fastest record ever made.

"All the songs were written on one synthesizer and an old guitar I rediscovered. I thought, if I can't make these work on these instruments then

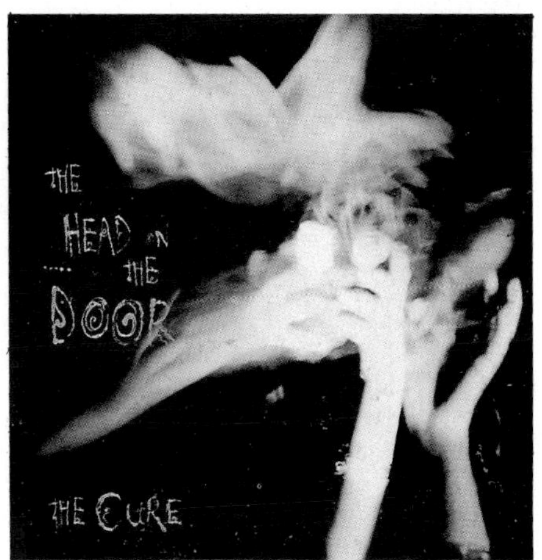

they won't have strong enough characters when it comes to record them for real. They all sounded quite different because I'd add my voice doing these ridiculous ideas for horn parts and there's a whole load of priceless cassettes with me imitating whole orchestras on them. Then we got Simon in and we all went into this demo studio and fell about laughing at these cassettes for a day."

Around the same time, Robert lets readers of *Just 17* into the secret of his increasingly disheveled appearance. "I don't worry too much about [it]. I mean, I haven't washed my hair for three and a half weeks . . . I always use gel, not hairspray. It's called KMS or something and it comes with hexagrams on. It's got the most glue-like consistency of anything I've ever come across. I back comb it a lot too. I did use mousse for a while but it used to drip onto my nose in big globs when I was on stage, which was disgusting."

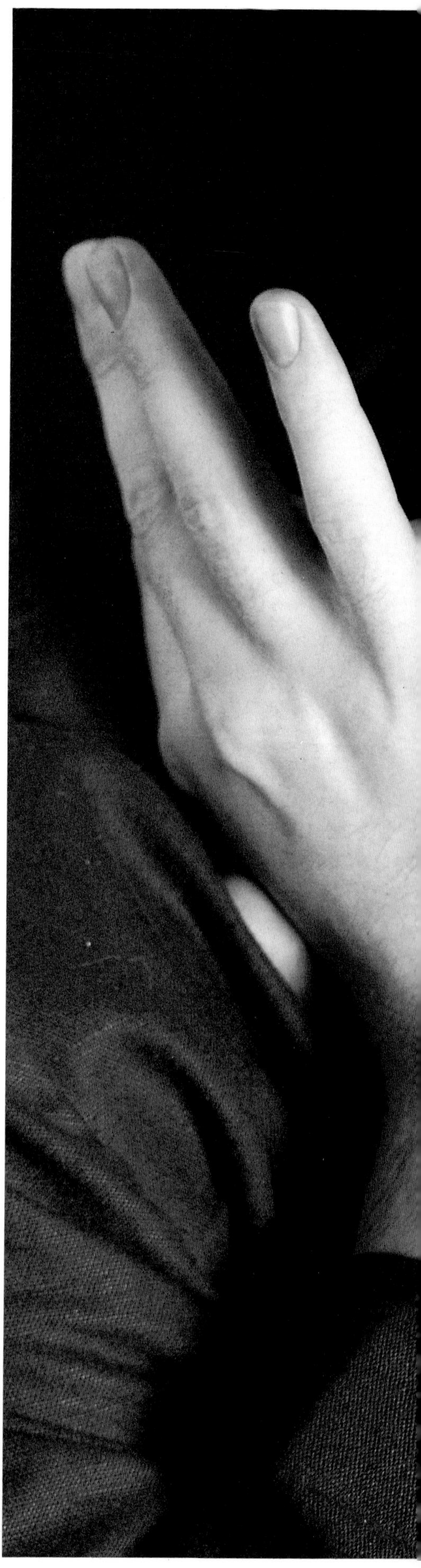

The Cure

The Cure

On stage at the Brighton Centre, September 1985. After this gig NME's reviewer commented: "I wouldn't like to be washed up on a desert island with this boring old sod."

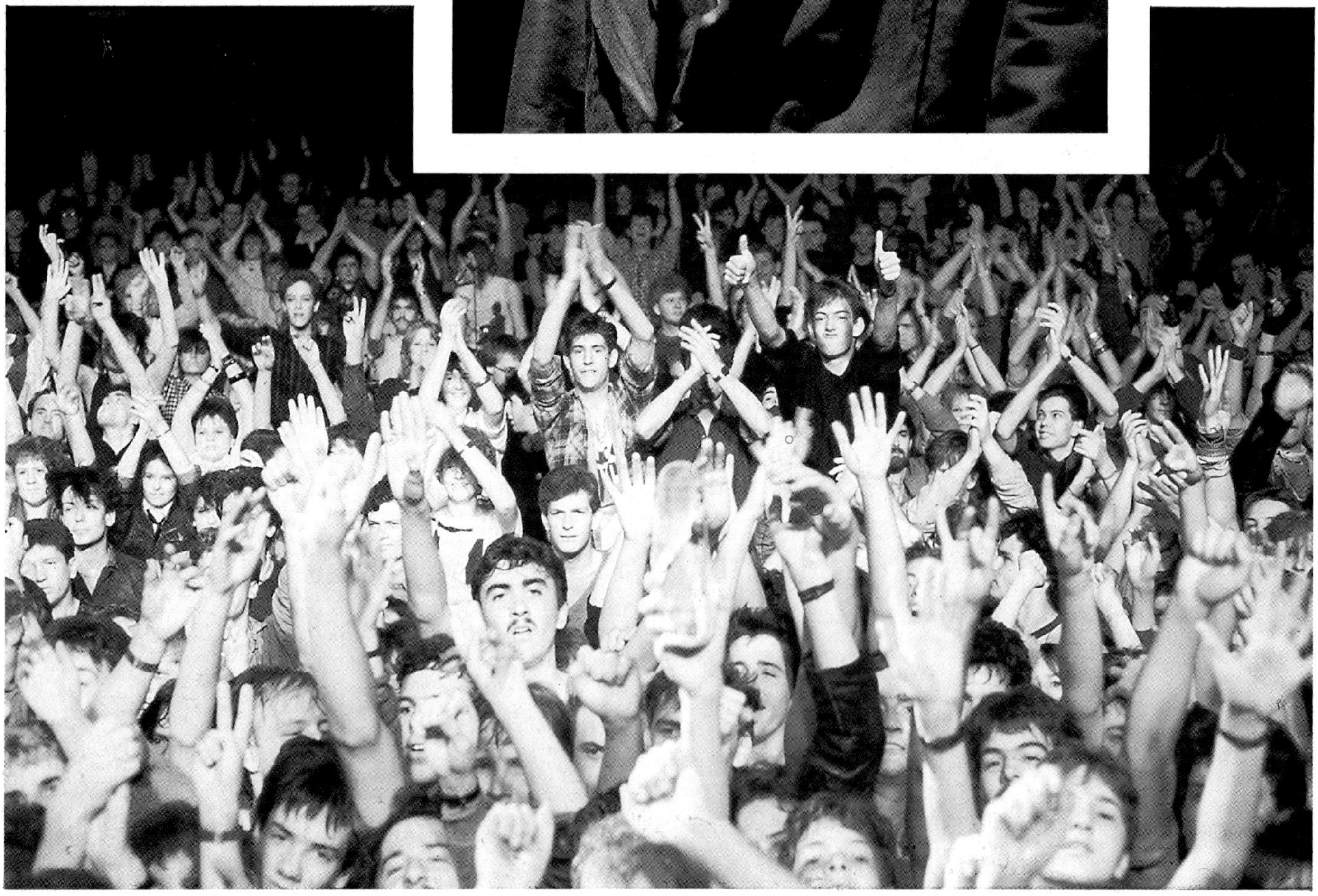

Left to right: Boris Williams, Robert, Porl, Simon and Lol.

24 AUGUST 1985

"A lot of people think 'Love Cats' was our first record, and that's fine because it gives us freedom that otherwise wouldn't be there."

Robert tells *Sounds* he is currently at work on his autobiography. "It should be out in April. I'm on page five at the moment. A French girl from a national newspaper is doing the interviews for me. That's really weird, listening to the thoughts of the people who were involved at the time. They've got really different interpretations of what my motives were and what they got out of it. It's really odd from people you think you know." He adds, "I used to write pieces for this Dutch magazine called *Oor*. I used to write arty pieces, about Christmas and things, and make up English words and they'd write and say 'We can not find this word in the dictionary, could you please translate?"

SEPTEMBER 1985

A new single is released from the album, 'Close To Me'/'A Man Inside My Mouth'. It is the first time The Cure have ever lifted two singles from one album, although 'Close To Me' is remixed, with added brass.

"I've always said we'd never release two singles off an album. But I was tempted because all the band were saying that if we release it it will get to number one." The accompanying video, which features the entire band crammed into a wardrobe which topples over a cliff ranks amongst the finest of the entire year. Three empty wardrobes were thrown from Beachy Head in the course of filming, and a local fire crew obliged by filling one with water, whilst the band lay inside. Unfortunately, the water had been sitting in the engine for some six weeks beforehand, "so we were all violently sick the next day."

And talking of wardrobes . . . *Record Mirror* asks Robert who are the musical skeletons in his closet? "I make up cassettes for when we're on tour, either for private use or for Club Smith use. This time around there's a sixties cassette with people like Mary Wells and Martha Reeves on it. Then there's a seventies tape with Lieutenant Pigeon and The Sweet, a disco tape with Anita Ward and Evelyn 'Champagne' King and then there's a psychedelic tape with Jimi Hendrix. There's even a heavy metal tape with the Pink Fairies and snatches of Alex Harvey, though he's not heavy metal."

8 SEPTEMBER 1985

The latest Cure tour begins at St. Austell Coliseum. The soundcheck reveals a few more of Robert's musical predilections; Gary Glitter's 'Do You Wanna Touch Me', The Kinks' 'You Really Got Me' and Hawkwind's 'Silver Machine', "Because this bloke who does our lights is completely deranged and whenever we play that one he's immediately transported back 20 years. He has flashbacks and starts doing the light show."

The Cure

At The Saint in New York City on a promotional trip for 'Standing On A Beach' and 'Staring At The Sea'.

9 SEPTEMBER 1985
Poole Arts Centre.

10 SEPTEMBER 1985
Shepton Mallet.

12 SEPTEMBER 1985
Wembley Arena.

14 SEPTEMBER 1985
Brighton Centre. "Robert Smith – he's so grim! Robert Smith – he's a bit overweight! God, I wouldn't like to be washed up on a desert island with that boring old sod! He's always moaning." (*New Musical Express*).

"I think the Brighton Centre is a very nice place . . . but as a place to go and see The Cure it's just not right. Bands like U2 and Simple Minds are perfect for this type of arena, their music is big, loud and anthemic and it doesn't take them long to have everyone singing along. The Cure aren't that sort of band. Their tunes are decidedly offbeat and weird. You listen and you wonder; you definitely don't scream. Their ideal venue would be a disused broom cupboard in a house at least 200 years old. There'd be a family of bats snuggled in a corner and a vaguely disgusting smell. Oh well, you can always imagine it . . . " (*No.1*).

16 SEPTEMBER 1985
Whitley Bay Ice Rink.

17/18 SEPTEMBER 1985
Apollo, Manchester.

20 SEPTEMBER 1985
NEC, Birmingham.

21 SEPTEMBER 1985
Queens Hall, Leeds.

22 SEPTEMBER 1985
Playhouse, Edinburgh.

28 SEPTEMBER 1985
The Cure cross the Atlantic for their next US tour, a jaunt which climaxes in a sold out engagement at the Radio City Music Hall, New York.

OCTOBER 1985

"Drinking is recreational. I used to get drunk on my own a lot but I don't any more. To use Dylan Thomas as an example, who ended up killing himself through drink, he did it just because it's good fun. I'm not sure it's the same in the latter stages of addiction. I imagine he drunk for three reasons. One because it's fun, two because you become almost mythical, it's like you become a legendary drinker which is an idea you can become addicted to, and the third reason is probably because in the latter stages of addiction you don't have much choice at all. I'm almost an alcoholic now, I haven't had one night this year when I haven't been drunk – a sad admission, I suppose."

Robert tells *The Face* he is writing a book of short stories – with no endings – called 'The Glass Sandwich', claims he would rather be a footballer than an existentialist and reveals, "I don't put my lipstick on properly because people would think I was doing it for reasons of vanity whereas I do it for reasons of theatricality. I used to wear red lipstick all around my eyes and all around my mouth when we were on stage (during the Pornography Tour) so that I'd sweat and it'd all run so it would look like someone had punched me in the mouth and my eyes were bleeding. I had to stop it though, because my eyesight started to suffer."

19 NOVEMBER 1985

The Cure play the Camden Palace in aid of the charity, MENCAP. Part of the show is broadcast live by BBC TV's Old Grey Whistle Test.

DECEMBER 1985

The Cure play a handful of shows in France. Meanwhile, Robert makes his début on the BBC TV Oracle service with a home-made cocktail called . . . Oracle. The ingredients form the initials – Orange juice, Rum, Apple slices, Calvados, Lemon juice, Everything mixed up. It tastes horrible. He also admits, in the press, that he has taken to lying in interviews. "I really hate being in the company of people who take themselves seriously. I always have done, but it's becoming pathological now. I can't stand people who sit and talk to me in a very serious way. When I go abroad I'll do three interviews in one country and give three different answers to all three, knowing that many people will read all of them and they won't be able to take you seriously because the whole thing is so absurd."

The Cure

MARCH 1986

Robert remixes 'Boys Don't Cry' and records a new vocal (so he won't have to mime to the old, higher-pitched one when the track is released as a single), as a taster for a forthcoming Cure compilation album. He and Tim Pope also put together an accompanying collection of Cure videos. Michael Dempsey is seen, in silhouette, playing with Robert and Lol in the video for the single.

APRIL 1986

'Close To Me' is challenging for the top of the French chart and The Cure return across the channel for an appearance on the French TV show, Champs Elysée, a programme which Lol describes as "Wogan and Top Of The Pops rolled into one." Porl and Boris are both on holiday, so Lol mimes drums, while his flatmate, Martin, plays keyboards.

The band express to *Record Mirror* their love of French audiences. "Thirty-seven people on the guest list and most of them under two," announces Robert, and while he reveals the band have probably met "about 1,000 people in every audience we play," Simon claims to have slept with half of them.

"The people who do talk to you are usually the last people you want to talk to you. Even when you're unknown the people who try to get back-stage are either trying to blag a free drink or they're so forward . . . I never went backstage when I went to see people except once, for Psychedelic Furs. And I tried to get backstage once for The Bunnymen but they wouldn't let me.

"If you're out you might go up to someone and say 'I liked your last record', but it's a bit different to going up to someone and saying 'I must give you my soul.' Usually their motives are very sound, but it just becomes very trying somehow."

"Quite simply, The Cure are the biggest thing to happen in France since Joan Of Arc's heart refused to burn at Rouen." (*Record Mirror*).

At the end of the month the revamped 'Boys Don't Cry' is released, backed by two tracks from the vaults – 'Do The Hansa', a lament for Easy Cure's first record company, and 'Pillbox Tales', taken from one of the Hansa demos. In America, 'Let's Go To Bed' is chosen as the A-side, with 'Boys Don't Cry' relegated to the flipside.

4 APRIL 1986

Jeanette Landray, now lead singer with Kiss That, confesses, "I couldn't sing when I did The Glove. It was all a con."

25 APRIL 1986

Greenpeace's week-long Soundwaves benefit ends with The Cure headlining the Royal Albert Hall. They perform 'Faith' for the first time since 1982 and Robert admits later, "I was crying through it. It's like rereading a page from your diary, like Christmas Eve 1975, and all the hopes you had. When I hear it I have to stop listening. I wish everything I did had such a strong effect on me."

"The Cure . . . have turned full circle and retraced in the wink of a shadowy eye the traumas of the last seven years, to end up not far from where they came in. There's little difference between a latterday pop classic like 'In Between Days' and a hitherto almost undiscovered, and now repolished gem such as 'Boys Don't Cry'" (*Melody Maker*).

"I've liked The Cure ever since they started, ever since 'Love Cats'," (Fan outside the Royal Albert Hall).

26 APRIL 1986

Robert: "If I ever read an interview with Morrissey – if I ever did, I don't think I've read one because he's such a boring bastard – but if he's going to say 'Life is cak' then, you think, 'Kill yourself or I will', because it's the same for everyone.

"Things generally are absurd and pretty awful most of the time, but I'm in a better situation than anyone I know so it seems two-faced of me to walk around moaning. Everyone in any room I'm ever in is going to die the same as I am so there's no point in bleating about it."

MAY 1986

'Standing On A Beach', which brings together all of The Cure's 13 singles to date, is released. Robert: "We've come to the end of our Polydor contract and if they don't release it with our blessing they'll release it anyway. And if we have any more singles it'll have to be a double album, which would be rather tedious." The cassette version brings together 12 Cure B-sides.

"The most amazing thing for me about what The Cure does is there is nothing in what we've done that I would do differently. I would do it differently if I did it all now, but there's nothing I would change from when it was done at the time."

"A chronological retrospective of all 13 of The Cure's singles is evidence that time has been kind to Robert Smith because he's always been so acutely aware, in awe and afraid of it. 'Standing On A Beach' is a very great record, a tipsy captain's log of a band all at sea because, after all, aren't we all?" (*Melody Maker*).

Simultaneously, 'Staring At The Sea', the video compilation, also appears, bringing with it new videos for the band's first three singles, plus footage both from The Bandstand in Crawley, shot by Robert's dad, and from the 1979 Reading Festival. Says Robert, "It's incredible how our faces change. It's not just that I'm fatter – I look a completely different person.

"I'm not a natural performer at the best of times. When I get lost in it I can be – but in a video, the atmosphere is too contrived. I don't really see myself in videos. I can see why I do it – it's the easy way out. In 'Love Cats' and 'The Walk' I wanted to get away from the way people have become accustomed to seeing me. Our early videos are very much what people expected The Cure to be like – 'A Forest' and all that. But if I continued in that vein it would get really tedious.

"The first videos we did were hilarious. We thought we were apart from image building so we stood in front of the camera looking like very bored people, which we were. Now we're well known for videos, thanks to Tim Pope. He translates our ideas really well. I'm a lot happier now and it shows."

"In the space of one hour Robert Smith changes from a fresh faced clean cut youth into the shambling figure of today." (*Smash Hits*).

"What makes it different from your average run of the mill video? Well I'll tell you. Haircuts. In the end, it's the sheer joy of watching sprouting locks on the move, particularly in the case of singer Robert Smith. First off it all looks quite normal if a little ruffled, but by the time they get round to 'Love Cats' and 'The Caterpillar', we are talking major hair dos. And very exciting it is too." (*Video World*).

Also this month, Robert flies to America to help promote both the compilations and a new tour, planned for July. "If I had to be in a group I'd be in this particular group because everything about it is really good."

Robert and Simon on stage at the Greenpeace Concert at London's Royal Albert Hall, April 1986.

15 MAY 1986
Having appeared on Dutch TV, performing 'Boys Don't Cry' and 'Close To Me', The Cure return to England to find 'Boys Don't Cry' standing at number 23 in the chart, and an invitation for The Cure to appear on Top Of The Pops. In the taxi on the way down to the studios, Robert claims, he was actually recognised by the cabbie. "You're that Boy George aren't you. Admit it."

"It's a little known fact, but one that Smith's perversely proud of, that The Cure have never appeared on the show and gone up the next week. Everyone else is guaranteed a leap of some sort or heads will roll around the marketing departments. But The Cure only have to stand there looking glum, or worse, distracted, and the particular single they're having to flog is destined to hurtle back down the charts with an anvil round its neck. Very strange." (*Melody Maker*).

In the event, the single actually goes up the chart the following week – one place.

16 MAY 1986
The Cure headline the Dutch Pink Pop Festival.

22 MAY 1986
The band travel to Venice aboard the Orient Express for a gig in Verona. When local fire chiefs cancel the show the trip becomes a brief holiday. BBC TV's Whistle Test accompany the band as far as Dover, filming an interview for broadcast later.

31 MAY 1986
Melody Maker invites Robert to offer his opinions on England's chances in the forthcoming football World Cup. He concludes, "The England team should be a combination of real bastards at the back and almost like effeminate gods at the front. Sadly it isn't." He admits, "I don't honestly think England will win the World Cup. Obviously I'd like it if they did but then Bobby Robson would be idolised and have the job for life and I'd hate that because I think he's a really cak manager – always have done. Let's face it, Ipswich were really dull. I wish I was Scottish for this World Cup."

JUNE 1986
Work begins on demos for the next Cure album, tentatively titled '1,000,000 Virgins'. The schedule is interrupted only by a handful of European festival engagements and Robert's fascination with the on-going World Cup Finals. *Sounds* ask him what is important to him at this minute? "That Glen Hoddle performs well in the World Cup and that England at least make it to the semi-finals."

14 JUNE 1986
Nürburgring, Germany. "We had five suits made

each, so that wherever we go we look similar. It's so we don't lose each other. A bit like wearing a yellow flag above your head. Who's in the band this week? Ah, he must be – he's got a suit on."

15 JUNE 1986
Munich.

18 JUNE 1986
The Cure appear on French television, an engagement which Robert only agrees to fulfil when he is promised it won't clash with the England v Paraguay match in the World Cup.

21 JUNE 1986
The Cure make only their second major UK appearance of the year at the Glastonbury CND Festival. "I still think the idealism involved in nuclear disarmament is laudable, but the knowledge to create the bomb is there and there's nothing we can do to take that away. Nuclear disarmament is really a very naïve dream. Nevertheless The Cure are still playing Glastonbury because there always has to be a level of public and private awareness, otherwise people in power become too complacent."

6 JULY 1986
Great Woods Centre, Mansfield. The first night of The Cure's American tour. Afterwards, Lol downs a bottle of Armagnac brandy and passes out, a comatose figure who is wheeled around the hotel lobby on a baggage trolly by the rest of the band. From there he is deposited in his room, from whence he telephones his girlfriend in LA and falls asleep with the receiver in his hand. His phone bill the following morning is for $1,500. Chris Parry announces that The Cure's only reason for existing is to kill Lol.

This, claims *Melody Maker*, is quite plausible. In Orange, Texas, Robert and Simon form the Lone Star White Protection Society and dedicate themselves to stop Lol smoking – by sticking all his cigarettes to a tree with masking tape. A note inside Lol's cigarette packet reads, "We warned you, dark boy. Regards, LSWPS."

The tour ends in New York, where Robert outrages the Radio City audience with the new haircut which has passed all but unnoticed elsewhere around the continent. "I was fed up with people saying 'God, how did you get your hair like that?' So before I went to America I thought 'I'll get you' and I had it cut off. The paradox, of course, is that now people talk about the hair even more. It's all they talk about. Everyone hates it. I hate it most. It's the most unattractive haircut. I just about recognise myself in the mirror now it's grown a little. Still, it makes no difference to me and, if it does to other people, well I hope they die."

Whilst in the US, Robert is interviewed by *Rolling Stone*. "I don't think I'm more depressed than anyone else I know. I'm not really obsessed with death [although] everything I do has the tinge of the finite, of my own demise. At some point you either accept death or you just keep pushing it back as you get older and older. I've accepted it."

AUGUST 1986

The Cure play a string of festivals in Spain and France. The last, on August 9, at the Roman Amphitheatre in Provence, is filmed in its entirety by Tim Pope, the first rock concert at the venue since Dire Straits two years previous.

"We wanted to film it . . . because every concert we do now reaches a point that has seemed unattainable in the past and I wanted it captured for ever, before we move on or give up. I don't think it's a risk working with Pap because he isn't really a director. We could have got in some proper director to make a film of any old concert but he wouldn't know what the band was about and I want this to be a Cure film about The Cure." Later, Robert claims to have been offered a film role, starring opposite Natassia Kinski. "I turned it down . . . she's not my type of woman."

Tim Pope:"This one's absolute psychedelic madness." To heighten the obvious comparisons with Pink Floyd's Live At Pompeii, the band play 'Set The Controls For The Heart Of The Sun' at soundcheck. And, reports *Melody Maker*, they play it perfectly.

"The risks, of course, are many. Because of the limited budget, all the live filming had to be done on Saturday, at the concert, with close-ups following during Sunday's mock up. Rain on one or both days would have scuppered the whole thing – £150,000 literally down the drain because they couldn't comprehend their cheapest insurance quote: £50,000. It didn't rain until Monday." (*Melody Maker*).

From here the band take a brief holiday in Toulon, then head into a studio in Oraguinon to continue work on the new album. The sessions eventually end up in Miravel, where the bulk of the new album is recorded (one number, 'I Want To Be You', has already been ushered into the live set). Now titled 'Kiss Me Kiss Me Kiss Me', the set swiftly proves such an awesome project that it quite naturally develops into a double set. "As we're recording out of the country, away from the distractions, it'll just be us and the Mrs Blokeys so it'll probably turn out to be a very odd album, for a change."

Producer David Allen says, "Working with The Cure I basically take the backing tracks as is, unless something really isn't working. It's hard to know what will and what won't work before you've heard the vocal line. With Robert you're working with someone who's made 10 albums and had a career since 1977, so I have great respect for him and confidence in his ability to come up with something good whenever he comes up with it. I think he wrote a lot of the melodies and lyrics actually at Miravel, although he tends to play things quite close to his chest, and you never quite know what stage he's at with a song.

"All the backing tracks and most of the guitar and keyboard overdubs were done at Studio Miravel, in the south of France. It has one large wooden room that's really quite dead, and a large concrete room . . . that used to be a storage room and is totally trash metal live. With 'Head On The Door' we used a wide variety of different kits and acoustics to create a totally different drum sound for each track. That was a very interesting process to go through, but it was such a pain in the arse to do that so we wanted it to be easier for this album. So we set up two kits, one of which was a dead, natural kit in the wooden room. Then we decided which tracks suited which basic drum sound."

Also during their French sojourn the band appear on national television performing 'Boys Don't Cry' in drag. From Studio Miravel the band move to Compass Point for three weeks. According to David Allen, "As it turned out we had such a limited time that we were doing two mixes a day, and so we booked more time at ICP Studios in Brussels to finish off a few weeks later."

28 SEPTEMBER 1986

A special showing of 'Staring At The Sea' at the London ICA terminates their season of rock videos.

Robert, having re-assessed the Barnet.

'87

JANUARY 1987

'Kiss Me Kiss Me Kiss Me' is completed at ICP in Brussels. All but two of the Compass Point mixes are remixed, and a few lines of vocal are re-recorded. The band then relocate in Eire, to begin rehearsals for their first South American tour.

MARCH 1987

The South American tour kicks off at the Buenos Aires Football Stadium. One hundred fans are arrested in the scuffle to gain admission to the 20,000 seater venue.

From here the band move on to Brazil, for eight shows, then spend much of the summer touring the United States. "I'm worried about us losing our edge. One of the things that's depressing me is the type of people that like The Cure now. Like, say, in California. It's like, if we sell a million records in America we're treated the same way as all the other groups who sell that. And if we don't have any distinctive qualities apart from my hairstyle there's no easy way out. And so I have to start talking about issues that people don't really want to hear about.

"We're not allowed on the Tonight show or the Joan Rivers Show. We're subversives because we're punks! We might set fire to the studio. We don't wanna help anyone. They actually told us in a telex memo that we were a 'punk group' and so we're not suitable for their audience."

10 APRIL 1987

'Why Can't I Be You'/'A Japanese Dream' is released. According to producer Dave Allen, "[it] was always a contender because it's short and up-tempo [although] it wasn't until much later that Robert picked it out as a single. Robert doesn't have any rules about what makes a good single, he'd release anything if he liked it enough."

The video is shot at the MTM Studios in Bray, a fancy-dress extravaganza which has Robert complaining, "I always thought I was destined for great things, but look at me! I'm in the scruffiest, laziest group in the world, dressed up in a fucking animal suit." Tim Pope, meanwhile, announces, "This is it! This is the video I've always wanted to make. The Cure DANCING! I can't believe I'm seeing this! They're FINISHED!"

23 APRIL 1987

The Cure In Orange, Tim Pope's 90-minute film of the French festival date is premièred at the Odeon, Marble Arch.

22 MAY 1987

'Kiss Me Kiss Me Kiss Me' released. Robert chose the title because he wanted a picture of his mouth on the cover. "It was really the desire to swallow people. The idea of drowning them rather than kissing them." Of the record itself, he says, "It sounds more real (than 'Head On The Door'). That was a very constructed album. I sort of sacrificed any inspiration that could have come out of the five-piece for the sake of getting the record done because there were so many things to be done after it. It's relaxed in that it's sure. It's the first time we've been a group since 'Pornography', when we could just sit down and play and I'd look at Lol or Simon and know what they meant. 'Shiver And Shake' and 'The Kiss' are really close to 'Pornography'. They would've got on ('Pornography') if I'd written them at the time because they are the horrible songs I was looking for then, but couldn't manage.

"'Fight' is the weirdest Cure song that we've ever done. It's like an anthem . . . it's the first one I've ever sung expressing the idea that other people should get up and do something. 'Pornography' was the opposite of that. I'd never have dreamed of doing a song like 'Fight' then – 'Give In' would have been more like it."

Producer Dave Allen says, "The band had written about 40 songs between them. So they did a couple of demoing sessions and ended up with

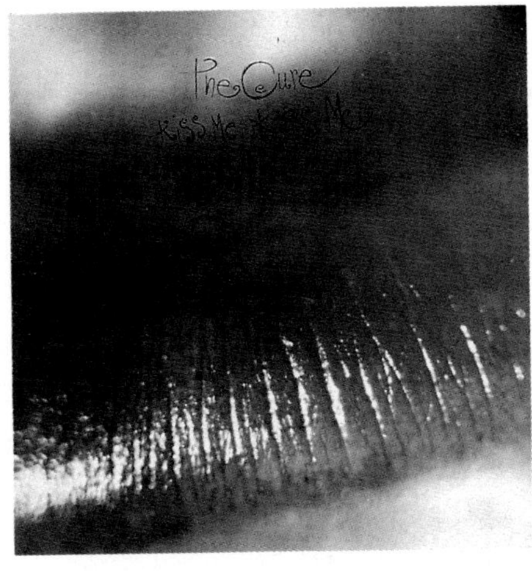

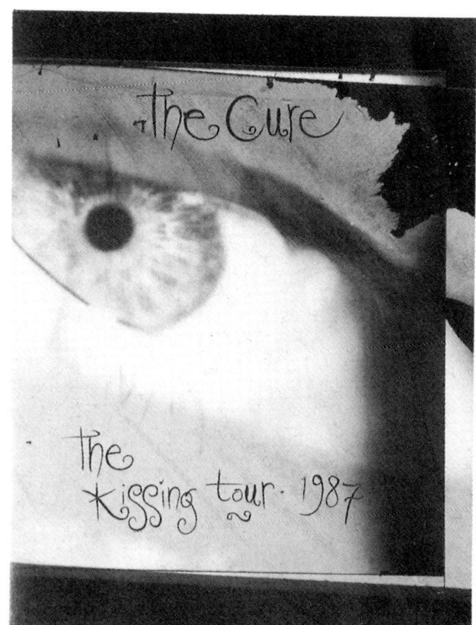

32 songs that were possibles for the record, 26 of which we finally recorded backing tracks for. We recorded all the backing tracks without me or most of the rest of the band knowing what was going to go over the top of them. All the instrumental arrangements were finished before any vocals were put down and I think 23 were completely finished with vocals and everything, 18 of which finally went on the album." Of these, three are written by Porl, two by Simon, the first time The Cure have recorded non-Smith compositions.

JUNE 1987
'Catch'/'Breathe' released as a single.

SEPTEMBER 1987
'Just Like Heaven'/'Snow In Summer' released as a single. Robert: "I went to the South Dublin coast for two weeks, I'd go out by the sea each morning and sit by the rocks. When I was younger it used to feel really inspired. And this time I actually felt really dead."

Around the same time Robert decides he wants to record a solo album "of whimsical songs." Lol immediately objects. According to Simon he fears it will make him look like the Andrew Ridgeley of the group – to which Robert retorts, "If he was as good as Andrew Ridgeley I'd invite him to play on it." He continues, "Lol, of course, immediately wants to do a solo album of his own. What's he going to do – an album of cycling or something?"

22 OCTOBER 1987
The Cure's Honeymoon Tour kicks off in Oslo. The band is now a six-piece, following the recruitment of keyboard player Roger O'Donnell. Most recently he has been touring with Psychedelic Furs, but tells *Sounds* he hated "every fucking minute of it." Writer Robin Gibson continues, "Roger is glad to be in The Cure. At least he gets in the photographs."

"One of our favourite occupations when we're abroad is to read the German equivalent of *Smash Hits*. You could seriously laugh yourself insensible at the people who are in it. Like, most of the people in groups with 'Hunky' written underneath are grotesque. I mean, one of the three in A-Ha looks like he's seriously sub-normal. The thin kiddie. He looks mental.

"My idea of hunkiness is Simon. Before, when it was just me, Lawrence and Simon in the group no-one ever bothered about what we looked like, which was fine. Now we have to, otherwise it looks like The Village People. If we let everyone wear what they wanted to wear Lol would certainly arrive in something rather ridiculous."

23 OCTOBER 1987
Stockholm. "I try to do things out of the ordinary. In Scandinavia I got up at 8.30 in the morning and just went out and watched people going to work. And that made me feel really happy. To see how other people felt, and knowing they'd have no release from it all day! I had some coffee and toast in this dingy cafe and thought, I am so *happy*."

24 OCTOBER 1987
Copenhagen.

25 OCTOBER 1987
Hamburg.

26 OCTOBER 1987
Berlin.

Montreux, May 1987.

28 OCTOBER 1987
Cologne.

29 OCTOBER 1987
Frankfurt.

30 OCTOBER 1987
Bremen.

1/2 NOVEMBER 1987
Brussels. "The show lurches very close to the sluggish lowest common denominator *stadiumism* of U2 and Simple Minds, but where The Cure preserve their dignity and pay homage to the essential illusions of rebellion is in the vicious, positively squirming, nooks and crannies of those cute rolling staccato songs." (*Melody Maker*).

3 NOVEMBER 1987
Louvain.

4/5 NOVEMBER 1987
Rotterdam. Back home the *Daily Mirror* reports, somewhat belatedly, that Robert and Mary have adopted two Guatemalan children each, paying for their education and upbringing. Back in July Robert told *International Musician*, "It's difficult to tell how they're doing really. They're still alive, they write happy letters and they draw very brightly coloured pictures. I suppose it means they're alright. But I wouldn't like to live in Guatemala, I don't see how you can be 'alright' in Guatemala.

"I very much doubt if they think of me very much. I never think of them as my children – they're only adopted in name. Your money pays for the education of the whole village, and you're given a picture and a name and an address to write to so it's more personal."

6 NOVEMBER 1987
Düsseldorf.

8 NOVEMBER 1987
Stuttgart.

9 NOVEMBER 1987
Zurich.

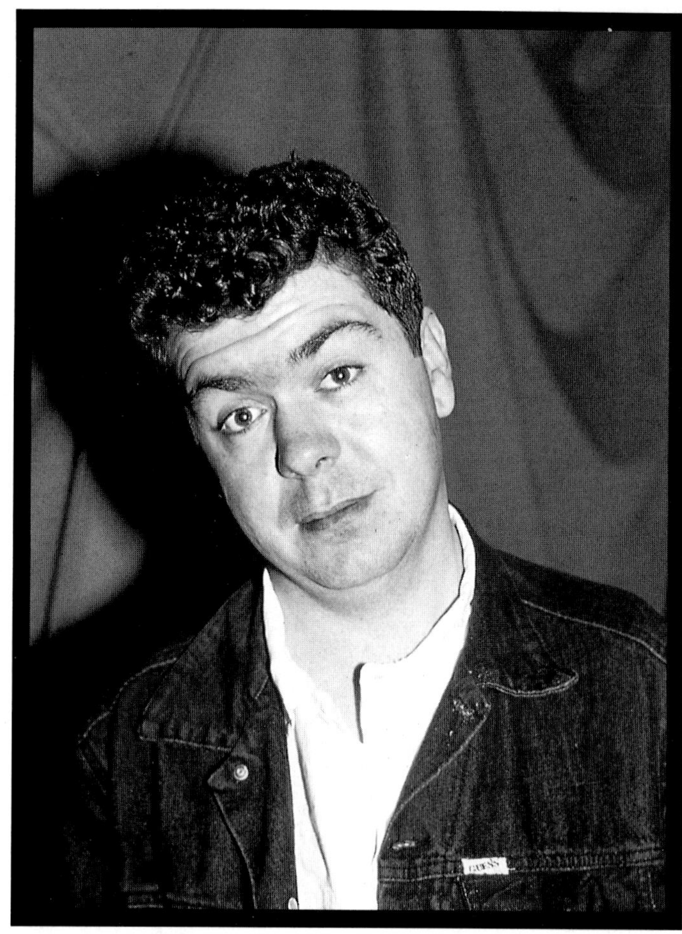

11-13 NOVEMBER 1987
Paris.

12 NOVEMBER 1987
The Cure Live In Orange video is released. "Exotic, hypnotic, packed with essential vitamin C, *The Cure In Orange* is The Cure playing with plenty of fizz and, with a running time of over two hours, it's no swizz. Featuring many of those nifty hit singles . . . as well as singer Robert Smith wearing a fetching shade of Boots No.7, this Tim Pope directed citrus classic is decidedly juicy." (*Video World*).

"Behind the band lies an arty backdrop, a little too clever for its own good but you can't criticise the sheer hard work on stage. Not one of Pope's best but as good a document of The Cure live as we'll get." (*Insight*).

Meanwhile, Barry Gibb of The Bee Gees, currently number one in Britain, confesses to being a Cure fan. The band, say *Melody Maker* are 'chuffed'.

The Cure

15 NOVEMBER 1987
Toulouse.

16 NOVEMBER 1987
Montpelier.

18 NOVEMBER 1987
Barcelona.

19 NOVEMBER 1987
Madrid.

20 NOVEMBER 1987
Valencia.

22 NOVEMBER 1987
Bilbao.

24 NOVEMBER 1987
Marseilles.

25 NOVEMBER 1987
Lyon.

27 NOVEMBER 1987
Rome.

29 NOVEMBER 1987
Modena.

30 NOVEMBER 1987
Florence.

1 DECEMBER 1987
Milan.

3 DECEMBER 1987
Bordeaux.

4 DECEMBER 1987
Nantes.

5 DECEMBER 1987
Robert: "The Cure on tour is a fascinating phenomenon . . . These are the main activities: Drinking. Saying 'Someone has never touched a drink in his life.' Watching old Dr Who videos. Lol-baiting. Arguing about the merits of compact discs and how the Luddites would smash them up. Crimping. Lol-baiting. Drinking. Phoning home. Anyone-baiting. Signing autographs. Trying to avoid signing autographs . . . "

6 DECEMBER 1987
NEC, Birmingham.

7/9 DECEMBER 1987
Wembley Arena. Robert: "I used to worry about the end of the group, or rather about the end of *me* in a group, about how addictive it was, but gradually the scales are tipping. It's becoming too much effort to be convincing onstage sometimes. Some nights I've noticed myself performing, like an animal, becoming the persona that exists in the videos. Dispassionate. Which my vanity enjoys, but which is clearly wrong. Cos I've grown up on stage singing things that take me into another world. It's been . . . a really strange way of . . . living."

BIRMINGHAM INTERNATIONAL
ARENA
NATIONAL EXHIBITION CENTRE
ARENA A

HARVEY GOLDSMITH
ENTERTAINMENTS
PRESENTS

THE CURE
IN CONCERT

DOORS OPEN 6:30PM

BLOCK
ARENA A
ROW
V
SEAT
17

£ 8.50

SUNDAY
6TH DEC
1987
8:00PM

ARENA A

Over and facing pages: And the future? Fatter all round perhaps.

Discography

SINGLES

Killing An Arab/10.15 Saturday Night
Small Wonder SMALL 11. December 1978.

Killing An Arab/10.15 Saturday Night
Fiction FICS 1. February 1979.

Grinding Halt/(No B-side)
Fiction white label demo, unreleased. April 1979.

Boys Don't Cry/Plastic Passion
Fiction FICS 2. June 1979.

Jumping Someone Else's Train/I'm Cold
Fiction FICS 5. October 1979.

A Forest/Another Journey By Train
Fiction FICS 10. April 1980.

Primary/Descent
Fiction FICS 12. April 1981.

Primary/Descent
Fiction 12" FICX 12. April 1981.

Charlotte Sometimes/Splintered In Her Head
Fiction FICS 14. October 1981.

Charlotte Sometimes/Splintered In Her Head/ Faith – live
Fiction 12" FICX 14. October 1981.

Hanging Garden/Killing An Arab – live
Fiction FICS 15. July 1982.

Hanging Garden/Killing An Arab – live/100 Years/ A Forest – live
Fiction 12" FICX 15. July 1982.

Hanging Garden/100 Years/A Forest/Killing An Arab
Fiction doublepack FICG 15. July 1982.

Lament
Flexi-Pop freebie. August 1982.

Let's Go To Bed/Just One Kiss
Fiction FICS 17. November 1982.

Let's Go To Bed/Just One Kiss
Fiction 12" FICX 17. November 1982.

The Walk/Upstairs Room
Fiction FICS 18. July 1983.

The Walk/Upstairs Room/Dream/Lament
Fiction 12" FICX 18. July 1983.

Love Cats/Speak My Language
Fiction FICS 19. October 1983.

Love Cats/Speak My Language/Mr Pink Eyes
Fiction 12" FICX 19. October 1983.

Caterpillar/Happy The Man
Fiction FICS 20. May 1984.

Caterpillar/Happy The Man/Throw Your Foot
Fiction 12" FICX 20. May 1984.

In Between Days/Exploding Boys
Fiction FICS 22. May 1985.

In Between Days/Exploding Boys/ A Few Hours After This
Fiction 12" FICX 22. May 1985.

Close To Me/A Man Inside My Mouth
Fiction FICS 23. September 1985.

Close To Me/A Man Inside My Mouth/Stop Dead
Fiction 12" FICX 23. September 1985.

Close To Me/New Day
Fiction 10" FICS 23. September 1985.

QUADPOS EP: A Night Like This/New Day/ Close To Me/A Man Inside My Mouth
US Elektra 066856. September 1985.

Boys Don't Cry/Pillbox Tales/Do The Hansa
Fiction FICS 24. April 1986.

Why Can't I Be You/A Japanese Dream
Fiction FICE 25. April 1987.

Why Can't I Be You/A Japanese Dream
Fiction 12" FICSX 25. April 1987.

Catch/Breathe
Fiction FICS 26. June 1987.

Catch/Breathe/Kyoto Song – live/ A Night Like This - live
Fiction 12" FICSE 26. June 1987.

Catch/Breathe/Chain Of Flowers
Fiction cassette FICSC 26. June 1987.

Just Like Heaven/Snow In Summer
Fiction FICS 27. September 1987.

Just Like Heaven/Snow In Summer/Sugar Girls
Fiction 12" FICS 27. September 1987.

ALBUMS

3 Imaginary Boys
Fiction FIX 001. Produced by Chris Parry. May 1979.
Foxy Lady/Meathook/So What?/Fire In Cairo/It's Not You/3 Imaginary Boys/10.15 Saturday Night/Accuracy/Grinding Halt/Another Day/ Object/Subway Song.

Boys Don't Cry
PVC 7916 – US compilation. Produced by Chris Parry. November 1979.
Boys Don't Cry/Plastic Passion/10.15 Saturday Night/Accuracy/Object/ Jumping Someone Else's Train/Subway Song/Killing An Arab/Fire In Cairo/Another Day/Grinding Halt/World War/3 Imaginary Boys.

17 Seconds
Fiction FIX 004. Produced by Robert Smith/Chris Parry. April 1980.
A Reflection/Play For Day/Secrets/In Your House/Three/The Final Solution/A Forest/M/At Night/17 Seconds.

Faith
Fiction FIX 006. Produced by Mike Hedges and The Cure. April 1981.
The Holy Hour/Primary/Other Voices/All Cats Are Grey/The Funeral Party/Doubt/The Drowning Man/Faith.

Faith/Carnage Visors
Fiction FIXC 6. May 1981.
Cassette only. As above plus film soundtrack.

Pornography
Fiction FIX 7. Produced by The Cure and Phil Thornally. May 1982.
One Hundred Years/A Short Term Effect/Hanging Garden/Siamese Twins/The Figurehead/A Strange Day/Cold/Pornography.

Boys Don't Cry
Fiction SPELP 26. August 1983.
UK release of PVC LP.

Japanese Whispers
Fiction FIXM 8. Tracks 1,2 produced by Chris Parry; 3-6 by Steve Nye; 7,8 by Phil Thornally/Robert Smith/Chris Parry. December 1983.
Let's Go To Bed/Just One Kiss/The Dream/The Upstairs Room/The Walk/Lament/Speak My Language/The Love Cats.

The Top
Fiction FIXS 9. Produced by Robert Smith/Dave Allen/Chris Parry. May 1984.
Shake Dog Shake/Birdmad Girl/Wailing Wall/Give It Me/Dressing Up/ Caterpillar/Piggy In The Mirror/The Empty World/Bananafishbones/ The Top.

Concert

Fiction FIXH 10. Produced by Dave Allen and The Cure. October 1984.

Shake Dog Shake/Primary/Charlotte Sometimes/The Hanging Garden/ Give Me It/The Walk/One Hundred Years/A Forest/10.15 Saturday Night/Killing An Arab.

Concert/Curiosity

Fiction FIXHC 10. "Made listenable by Phil Thornally." October 1984.

Cassette only. As above plus: Heroin Face/Boys Don't Cry/Subway Song/At Night/In Your House/The Drowning Man/The Funeral Party/ All Mine/Forever.

Head On The Door

Fiction FIXH 11. Produced by Robert Smith/Dave Allen/*Howard Gray). August 1985.

Inbetween Days/Kyoto Song*/
The Blood/Six Different Ways/Pushy*/The Baby Screams/Close To Me/A Night Like This*/ Screw/Sinking.

Standing On A Beach

Fiction FIXH 12. Produced as detailed above. May 1986.

Killing An Arab/Boys Don't Cry/Jumping Someone Else's Train/ A Forest/Primary/Charlotte Sometimes/The Hanging Garden/ Let's Go To Bed/The Walk/The Lovecats/The Caterpillar/In Between Days/Close To Me.

Standing On A Beach

Fiction FIXHC 12. Produced as detailed above. May 1986.

Cassette only. As above plus: I'm Cold/Another Journey By Train/ Descent/Splintered In Her Head/Mr Pink Eyes/Happy The Man/ Throw Your Foot/The Exploding Boy/A Few Hours After This/ A Man Inside My Mouth/Stop Dead/New Day.

Kiss Me Kiss Me Kiss Me

Fiction FIXH 13. Produced by Robert Smith/Dave Allen. May 1987.

The Kiss/Catch/Torture/If Only Tonight/We Could Sleep/Why Can't I Be You?/How Beautiful You Are/The Snakepit/Hey You!!!/Just Like Heaven/All I Want/Hot Hot Hot!!!/One More Time/Like Cockatoos/Icing Sugar/The Perfect Girl/A Thousand Hours/Shiver And Shake/Fight.

Limited edition orange vinyl mini album included with 'Kiss Me Kiss Me Kiss Me'.

Fiction FIXHA 13. Produced by Robert Smith/Dave Allen. December 1987.

A Japanese Dream/Breathe/Chain Of Flowers/Sugar Girl/Snow In Summer/Icing Sugar.

VIDEOS

All directed by Tim Pope except where noted.

10.15 Saturday Night (Piers Bedford)
Play For Today (Dave Hillier)
A Forest (Dave Hillier)
Other Voices (Bob Rickerd)
Primary (Bob Rickerd)
Charlotte Sometimes (Mike Mansfield)
Hanging Garden (Chris Gabrin)
Let's Go to Bed
The Walk
Love Cats
Caterpillar
In Between Days
Close To Me
Boys Don't Cry
Why Can't I Be You

Staring At The Sea

Full length collection. April 1986.

Killing An Arab/10.15 Saturday Night/Boys Don't Cry/Jumping On Someone Else's Train/A Forest/Play For Today/Primary/Other Voices/ Charlotte Sometimes/Hanging Garden/ Let's Go To Bed/The Walk/Love Cats/Caterpillar/In Between Days/Close To Me/A Night Like This.

The Cure In Orange

Concert film. November 1987.

Introduction/Shake Dog Shake/Piggy In The Middle/Play For Today/ A Strange Day/ Primary/Kyoto Song/Charlotte Sometimes/In Between Days/The Walk/A Night Like This/Push/A Hundred Years/A Forest/ Sinking/Close To Me/Let's Go To Bed/Six Different Ways/3 Imaginary Boys/Boys Don't Cry/Faith/Give Me It/10.15 Saturday Night/ Killing An Arab.

COLLABORATIONS

THE CULT HEROES

Single with Robert Smith

I'm A Cult Hero/I Dig You
Fiction FICS 6. December 1979.

THE GLOVE

Singles with Robert Smith

Like An Animal/Mouth To Mouth
Wonderland SHE 3. August 1983.

Like An Animal/Animal/Mouth To Mouth
Wonderland 12" SHEX 3. August 1983.

Punish Me With Kisses/The Tightrope
Wonderland SHE 5. November 1983.

Album with Robert Smith

Blue Sunshine
Wonderland SHELP 2. August 1983.

SIOUXSIE AND THE BANSHEES

Singles with Robert Smith.

Dear Prudence/Tattoo
Wonderland SHE 4. September 1983.

Dear Prudence/Tattoo/There's A Planet In My Kitchen
Wonderland 12" SHEX 4. September 1983.

Swimming Horses/Let Go
Wonderland SHE 6. April 1984.

Swimming Horses/Let Go/Humming Wires
Wonderland 12" SHEX 6. April 1984.

Dazzle/I Promise
Wonderland SHE 7. June 1984.

Dazzle/I Promise/Throw Them To The Lions
Wonderland 12" SHEX 7. June 1984.

Albums with Robert Smith.

Nocturne
Wonderland SHAH 1. November 1983.

Hyaena
Wonderland SHEHP 1. June 1984.

TIM POPE

Single with Robert Smith.

I Want To Be A Tree/Elephant Song
Fiction FICS 21. August 1984.

I Want To Be A Tree/Elephant Song/
The Double-Crossing Of Two Faced Fred
Fiction 12" FICSX 21. August 1984.